THEIR TANGO AND ANTARCTICA SECRETS

A Bi Wanderlust Romance

Sheila Hollihan-Elliot and Merlin Edward Angel

Palm Beach Press Inc - Black Swan Imprint

BLACK SWAN
IMPRINT

Dedicated to Black Swans everywhere

"Remember that you are a Black Swan."

NASSIM NICHOLAS TALEB, THE BLACK SWAN:
THE IMPACT OF THE HIGHLY IMPROBABLE

CONTENTS

CHAPTER 1

DISCOVERY
Donna Speaking

Antarctica. That's where I'm heading by three planes and a ship. My two-week reward for keeping my long ago promise. To protect my husband. Forever.

It hasn't been easy for anyone who crawls out from the attack. Immediately, mathematician Taleb identifies it as the unforeseen Black Swan event that changes everything. Launches our 21st Century. Replaces the ousted familiar world with this new one we invent rules to survive. Yet finally, 20 odd years later, in my own corner of this different world foisted on us, I secure agreements. How we three, my husband David, Tanya and I, can go forward, allowing murky love, yet still living within the rules that keep him from danger.

YAY.

Of course, now all I seek is relief. From negotiation. From worry. Even from my indispensable corporate job for a few days before returning to make sure our lives DO get better. I'll let loose, relax, and explore someplace new to give myself a little treat.

So I arrange possible vacation dates and apply as a "single needing roommate" for any two-week tours sponsored by the Met, Smithsonian, even my college alumnae office.

I'm thrilled to snag a last-minute opening in the 5-star "Discovery" Antarctica tour starting day after tomorrow. On the Swan Hellenic's Vega, their new luxury expedition cruise ship.

I look over the pdf brochure one more time, comforted that they turned their official black swan logo into a white swan on black background. I can hear in my mind how the meeting with the new private owners goes down:

"We WILL NOT use the black swan as a logo."

"Nobody knows Mr. Swan and his son started Swan Tours."

"We're targeting the diverse young 18-40 crowd – they aren't re-living the past and the young ones weren't even born by 9/11."

"Other clients will be well-heeled oldsters. We can't let them flock to competitors."

"OK, we'll make your 'black swan' deep deep purple – British Royal – and float it in white against a black background banner when we market for sales."

"Deal?"

"Deal."

After this daydream, I feel like a functioning anachronism. I'm only 42 but apparently no longer one of the desirable demographics. Funny, isn't it, how I'm not bothered. Free from being hustled.

I quickly notify HR of my leave-date. Call Tanya to come out to the apartment to take care of the cat Goldie and David, my husband, while I'm away.

I pack a small suitcase and carry-on with outdoor clothes and lots of sweaters – it is after all, January 1 that the plane leaves from JFK for Miami. Thank the heavens there are no visa requirements —just my passport I use for work anyway so it's always current.

"So where you headed, Donna?" my husband asks once more.

"Antarctica. You won't be alone—I already called Tanya. You'll be fine."

"It's getting dark. Turn on the lights."

I illuminate everything, including the bedroom, and turn in early. "I'm catching a 6:00 am plane. Sweet dreams."

Darn. In the morning, just as I dash to the cab, my husband throws a monkey wrench into my good mood. "We've got to resolve it, Donna. When you get back?"

"Sure, sure—of course." I don't even know what we must resolve—again. I'm never possessive of his dalliance, so who knows what it really is.

At Miami International Airport, I calm myself down enough to wait inside the glass terminal to board the flight to Buenos Aires, the sprawling *Río de la Plata* port city and capital of Argentina. That's where this tour officially begins.

Out of nowhere, a black limousine comes to an abrupt halt outside, and I see a scene like a cliché B movie. Six fit male uniformed bodyguards pile out. With exaggerated politeness, they open the door for a tall slim well-dressed gentleman in a dark tailored suit. Behind him is a younger man, shorter, toned and as well turned out, with the same crisp haircut though not peppered with areas of grey like the taller gentleman.

Both appear close. A wealthy father and son taking a trip together, I guess.

Father, son and half the bodyguards proceed toward the entry gate. Two others extract a Louis Vuitton suit bag and matching portmanteau wardrobe trunk from the limo's trunk.

The remaining bodyguard scowls at us passengers sitting in the public waiting area. He takes notes as if we are terrorists. Not to be intimidated by his arrogance, I grab my carry-on to start a checked passengers' line.

Mr. Arrogance rushes my new line and pushes me backward.

"Clear the way for esteemed gentlemen."

I push forward. "Shove off. This is my spot." That always works in New York City when I need to walk through a street brawl.

He shoves me back even harder. This time, as I try to keep from falling backward, I careen too far forward and land grabbing the legs of one of those "esteemed gentlemen".

Surprised, I tilt my head to stare up. I am awestruck by his black-flecked brown eyes, those lips, skin darkly tanned except for that white scar from the corner of his left eye to his prominent sculpted cheekbone.

I feel goosebumps crawl up my arm, unexpected, but his face is uncommonly beautiful. Intriguing, this scarred mystery man.

For an instant our eyes lock. Then like a schoolgirl, I feel I'm blushing. Embarrassed, I get myself up and step back.

I hear him speak to his son "So you won't change your mind?"

The son doesn't answer but turns and stomps out through the terminal's exit.

His smooth sexy voice could have made me swoon if it weren't for that head bodyguard quickly hustling the tall man onto the plane. All bodyguards follow him out of sight.

Still, my stomach finds a butterfly or two. A weird reaction I've ached for but never felt with anybody like this before. An interesting woman I'd notice, yet I'm suddenly intrigued by this mystery man?

When we land in Buenos Aires, the VIP's bodyguards take over the plane's exit and I have a tantalizing glimpse of that same "esteemed gentleman" as he leaves.

When the exit ramp clears, I'm back to the real world and scramble off the plane like a happy kid arriving at summer camp.

I'm shocked to find it's really hot. Of course I know that below the equator it's their summer, but wow, all those sweaters I jammed into my bag.

By 7:30 pm I collect the suitcase and look for a cab. Ezeiza International is half an hour outside Buenos Aires, so by now I am running late. The official start of the tour, the meet-and-greet, is scheduled for 8:00 pm, but I can't help pausing under the arched exit canopy with its fantasy blue lights the color of the Virgin's robe. The effect is magical. "This design should be awarded a medal," I shout to whoever else is hurrying to the taxi curb.

Pulling up to the Hotel *Palacio* is even more magical. "It was built by the Duhau Family last century to be their actual palace – it is not a stage set" I read from the tour agenda.

Let's face it, folks, a luxury tour is a luxury tour. It needs to have some glitz for the price.

At the meet-and-greet, tour members chat as waiters with bubbly champagne coupes circulate. "I'm Donna from NYC", I introduce myself to quite an international gathering of well-heeled elites.

By 9:00 pm, the tour leader starts her announcements in the *Posada* Ballroom set with chairs facing a projection screen. "You'll find your rooms have health and safety gear already placed on your luggage racks," she reads.

As we settle, I select my usual "moment's notice" problem-solver's corner chair nearest the door in the back row. I count the seated —99. One is empty. Too bad someone is missing this adventure.

"Madame Maccoy" the concierge calls in a low voice as he peers from the doorway. He's using the global protocol "Madame" as a term of respect no matter what country or language is spoken.

I step out and meet him.

"We processed your passport and apologize for the delay. Here is your room key for the hotel and cabin key for the ship. We do hope you enjoy your stay with us."

"By any chance do you know who my cabinmate is?"

"We are not privy to those records, Madame. As you know, we protect the privacy of elite tour members." Then he whispers, "Keep this to yourself, but I understand it's another Donna. I overheard the tour staff giggling about a last-minute passenger replacement–resulting in two Donna's in the same cabin."

"We meet back here at 8:00 am for breakfast," the tour leader concludes. "We'll announce then if weather conditions enable us to start south or if it must be an Argentina leisure day."

The audience groans at that suggestion. I've never been on a tour before, so I'm surprised by this obsessing on weather.

I make the way to my hotel room number through elegant halls decorated with paintings the likes of which I've seen only in museums. I reach The King Twin Suite. It sounds overly luxurious, but it is the right door number, so I try the key and it works. I step into an anteroom.

There on a luggage rack is my suitcase with my name taped to it. Next to it, a rack is piled with spiked metal trekking poles, boot crampons, wetsuit, and crowning it all, the status symbol orangey-red nylon explorer's jacket with my name embroidered over the heart.

Past this anteroom I see a bedroom with two regal looking twin beds canopied with satin swags and gauzy bed curtains. What an amazing way the *petit* nobility lived–and I suppose with enough money, we can still live this way.

Realizing my cabinmate hasn't arrived yet – that empty seat – I decide I'd like the bed by the window, fetch my silky red nightgown, and start off to find a tub for a soothing hot bath.

Too bad she's missing...if she doesn't get here soon, she might even miss the tour.

I hear someone gently open the door. I am sure I remembered to lock it. "Who's there? Donna, is that you?"

I glimpse a tall man entering the anteroom who seems vaguely familiar. Startled, I freeze.

What is he doing here? Did he enter the wrong room?

"Who are you?" I ask what seems an impossible dream mirage.

"Don't you know who I am?"

"No" I whisper...

CHAPTER 2

THE 100th TOURIST
Miguel Speaking

Walking in from the anteroom, I answer clearly, "My name is Don Miguel de Casas."

"What are you doing here? I'm supposed to have a cabinmate. You are an intruder," declares the tall slender woman, grasping a slinky red nightgown to her, now facing me. Could a retired NYC model be replacing Luis-Alfonso, who was supposed to be here with me?

She runs past me to the anteroom and speaks the name taped to my portmanteau wardrobe trunk. "Dona Casas?"

I chuckle. "'Dona' is not a real name. In my set, Don is the respectful way to say "Mister".

"I know that", she snaps. "And it's not funny, Miguel de Casas, if that's who you say you are."

She has something there. Could it be she's in the same line of work as me? For now, I'll ignore that possibility.

"I always stay in the King Suite when I visit Antarctica." I fib on the hotel, trying to soothe her.

"You've been to Antarctica before?" I can see she blurts it out and then tries to come up with how to get rid of me.

"Let me put you at ease. You have nothing to fear from me." I soothe again.

"That's not the issue. I have a reason not to be rooming with a man. It's called a husband."

"Would it help if I told you I have a reason not to room with a woman?"

"No."

"Think of this—you might be able to find another room in this hotel, but on this new ship to Antarctica, all rooms will already be occupied."

"You mean I am stuck with you?"

"That's hardly flattering, but yes."

"Hrmff" She huffs.

I watch her return to the bed by the window and make a show of selecting it by laying her nightgown over the fine linen counterpane. I can't help it. She deserves to be ruffled.

"That's my bed." I provoke in a bit of fun.

"Why?" I am surprised she didn't use her sassy "Shove off. This is my spot," from her Miami spat.

Now it is my turn. "Shove off. This is my spot." I tease again.

She recognizes her phrase and that breaks the ice. Grinning, she blushes, and I sense she is about to give up her refusal to room with me.

"Well as long as nobody ever hears about this."

Now I laugh. "I'm always under surveillance. Although a shared room with a so-called 'private person' can't be so nonchalantly bugged."

"So, I'm your protector now?" she retorts, looking more startled than I would expect from a lucky tourist who just got this last-minute ticket.

"If you put it that way, yes."

"Hrmff"

"So, Madame, tell me why you requested an unknown roommate."

"My husband doesn't travel, and I couldn't afford a double room for myself."

"Well then we're even—you keep me from surveillance bugs, and I enable you to take this tour."

She goes back to her appealing grin. "Yes sir, even Steven if you please–sir."

"By the way, I was joking, choose whichever bed you want."

The King Twin Suite has two separate bathrooms, where we

prepare for the night. And yes, she repeats her choice of what would have been my bed, the one by the window. Somehow that feels right, that in this very small way, we do have something in common.

By morning, the sunlight bathing her form is alluring. She reminds me of a child, excruciatingly thin, no makeup, brownish hair tousled with sleep. I do my morning ablutions with that sweet image stroking me as I shower.

"Ready to go down to breakfast?" she greets, having already finished her own morning routine.

"*Tout de suite*," I reply as I open the door. We walk out carefully. We do not accidentally touch each other.

At breakfast, we go to the buffet with the other members. I notice them loading their plates with American style layers of eggs, sausages, potatoes, even muffins and pancakes, yet Donna and I eat like hostages – mostly black coffee with a bit of nearly nothing and thus being quick, we return to the long table pretty much alone.

"Now I must show you something," she asserts.

Again, I feel that momentary jitter. Are we both trained in delivering messages?

She takes her iPhone and shows me her family.

First is a photo of a young man in an Air Force lieutenant's uniform. "My son Bruce just last week."

Then there is a boy with the same angular face. "And here 10 years ago at the local farm stand." This is an endearing framed drawing.

"My husband's an artist, but it's a May-December marriage. I get someone to stay in the apartment and look after him —and my cat —when I'm away for my job."

She closes her phone with "Or like now, this two-week adventure break from all that New York City striving."

She shows no photograph of that husband.

I look into her eyes. She returns my stare and nods "no". I understand that message. She just red-lined her cabinmate rule. For whatever reason, it means "hands off."

"Listen up, all" The tour leader announces through the mic. "Unfortunately, there are storms in the Drake Passage. So, we cannot go south yet."

Breakfasters groan. The leader performs with apparent surprise. I've seen these orchestrated delays in Buenos Aires before. Perhaps Argentina's unfortunate commission on the Antarctica tourism industry. We try to control it yet haven't found an investor to deal with our rampant inflation. No group is willing to build Argentine tour ships. A pity. So do we delay tours in our city, encouraging enjoyable and profitable events before they trundle south?

"Hence today is an at-leisure day—the concierge will have city maps, tickets to museums, a list of fashionable boutiques, and they can guide you to other events you might want to attend on your own. Please reassemble here at 8:00 am for breakfast and tomorrow's agenda."

To be honest, I am happy we will have a day off to explore Buenos Aires.

"Would you like to explore together?" my Hands-Off Cabinmate asks.

"Madame Maccoy, nothing could please me more." I say with a sweeping bow, my mock royal gesture.

"Let's run to the concierge and get those maps before we have to wait in line."

"No need. I know this city's secrets ... intimately."

CHAPTER 3

MRS CHIPPY
Donna Speaking

"Where would you like to explore?" Don Miguel asks as we leave the breakfast area.

"Sir, I leave that up to you, since you know this city's secrets so...intimately" I tease.

I'm glad he knows the city. It was all so sudden I didn't have time to research either Antarctica or Buenos Aires. Once I joined the meet-and-greet last night I thought we'd just overnight here and immediately be taking the next flight south to Port Ushuaia. Apparently not, a weather delay. Unexpected?

"But first I need to get something from our room," he says.

Curious, I ask if I can come along.

"Delighted again. You are always welcome." His voice is subtle and warm. He does seem to mean it.

Damn this bunch of hormones in me —early menopause is throwing me into what magazines call adolescent franticity, though all of this is new to me. I wasn't even like this when I was a teen—I didn't even like boys. And now this? Am I blushing again? Luckily, he's rushing ahead so he didn't see me thrilling to his being. I honestly don't trust this crazy attraction – it's not the real me.

By the time I catch up with him, the King Suite door is open and so is his portmanteau trunk. He takes a leather envelope and secretes it in the inside pocket of his elegant jacket.

As we are leaving, the hotel butler, who comes with this suite, asks for directives on our needs for the evening.

"Tuxedo black tie for late dinner and the lady will be wearing something newly purchased."

So that's how the wealthy live. This is turning out to be quite the adventure.

As we leave, Miguel says, "First I must drop off elements for something I want to order."

We stroll within the maze of the *Palacio's* formal gardens, and then walk a block further to a discreet private jewelry establishment.

"Is this your 'go-to' jeweler? Since I am actually doing this Explore Day–Sir—might I ask why not Cartier or Tiffany's?"

"Simple. Anyone with a bank account can buy the same things everyone buys. But a private jeweler will design something special to suit only one client—the equivalent of upscale fashion boutiques vs. *haute couture*."

At the jeweler's, I peek at what Miguel takes from the envelope. It's a sepia photograph of a tabby cat perching on a young man's shoulder. The handsome man who sports the cat looks somewhat like the son who refuses to accompany his father.

Not wanting to remind Miguel of a family tiff, I wait until we are outside to ask why he gave a picture of a cat and his son to the jeweler. He looks taken aback, pausing apparently to devise an answer.

"That's just Mrs. Chippy. She's the only cat to make it to Antarctica."

He didn't answer my "why", so I prompt "And?"

"There's a secret about her."

"Yes?" I wish to hear it now.

"Sometime I'll tell you. But not now."

I am disappointed and surprised he didn't mention his child. But it is, after all, an Explore Day. Despite my tingles and quickened breathing, in two weeks it will be a relief to go back to deciphering corporate politics, not Don Miguel's quirky effect on me.

"Of course. Let's explore—Sir."

All the tourist sites are within walking distance, sometimes far to be sure, from the exclusive *Recoleta* neighborhood of the *Palacio* and its impressive mansions.

The *Plaza de Mayo* in front of the pink *Casa Rosada*, the presidential palace, is eerily empty. "Today it is silent," he says. "But each Thursday at 3:30 pm, the *"Madres of the Disappeared"* trudge the circle, reminding with their white headscarves, that they will never absolve politicians of what they did. So many were lost in our coup."

I notice he says "our". I notice even more how passersby nod, as if he is someone important who warrants great respect.

Next, we walk to *La Recoleta*, the cemetery of the *Familias* Leading Families and nation's heroes, including the Duarte Family tomb containing Eva Perón. Years ago, I had cried and fallen in love with Evita and her Argentina, so I know there will be busses of tourists lined up to visit her here.

We stop at a butcher shop near the entry gate.

"My usual, but two bags." Don Miguel orders.

The counterman thanks him profusely for his generosity.

"What is that about?" I ask as he gives me my bag. His hand touches mine and feels like ice. Is his heart as cold? I peer inside the bag and see torn shreds of beef, like the smashed corpses in the attack. Is he as dangerous?

The second we enter the cemetery gate we are surrounded by cats.

"We believe these cats are poor souls who have lost their way to Heaven. It's our *Porteño*—people of the Port— tradition to feed them while they search for their God."

On the way to order a car for our next exploration, the front door of a gated Beaux Artes mansion opens, and a uniformed attendant runs toward us. "Don Miguel. Will you be staying?"

"Not today, but I do want the town car now. We will wait inside for it."

We walk into a tastefully decorated entry hall, and share a bench upholstered in Argentine flag *celeste* blue velvet gaufrage to wait.

"What is this place?" I ask.

"*El Cuartel*"

"Translate please."

"My home."

Something is fishy. Home should be *la casa*, like his name. I'm not even sure that is his name. I stare at him and plug *cuartel* into my phone's translator app. It comes up with *cuartel=barracks*.

"This home gives privacy," he tempts me to ignore the phone.

"Miguel, doesn't every home give privacy?"

"Not as I require …"

CHAPTER 4

MILONGA TANGO
Miguel Speaking

"Where shall I take you, sir?" asks the chauffeur as we slip into the back seat.

"Ezeiza, Terminal A."

"The airport? Why?" Donna seems worried.

"To show you something most travelers miss. Tell me, did you see a small sculpture on the airport's second floor as you exited the plane?"

"No. I was rushing to find a cab."

"When you view this art, Madame Maccoy, please tell me what you think of it. A close friend, a survivor, sponsored it."

I escort her to the Raoul Wallenberg memorial "Hero Without a Grave 1912—".

I can see she doesn't like the bronze—that had been my reaction too when I first beheld it.

She lingers on the plaque's words, and then the artist signature Beñat Iglesias Lopez. I remember my friend's search for a sculptor. Argentina tried so hard to develop its own art identity but raging inflation and poverty prevented it. One by one, artists barely surviving with brutal day jobs, fled to the different art capitals of the world. My friend finally gave up finding an Argentine sculptor and looked in New York City to find at least a Spanish one. So sad. Argentina spent last century trying to establish *Argentinidad* national culture, but everything thwarted it. Genocide, dictators, European immigrants who expect to leave as soon as they make their fortune, in the meantime creating an imitation Paris and her arts in Buenos Aires. So much wasted potential...only the native *Milonga* street dance —which promotors call the Tango—survives all this...

"It's solemn," she muses, "and quite last century's academic art style, like my husband teaches to eager housewives—"

Donna cuts herself off and seems embarrassed if she's saying too much.

"Please continue."

"It's only my opinion," she apologizes.

"No, I can see you have a clear vision, even if you are reluctant to share it."

Donna continues, "I think I know the name–isn't he the artist who displays such expressive sculptures in New York City parks?"

"There you have it. Yes, this was an early work, before he found his soul."

Soul again—lost soul cats, a soul-less artist searching for his soul. This is too heavy. I owe her to bring some lightness to our Explore-Day together.

"Now, Madame, to explore the city's nightlife, we need to outfit you as a mystery *Porteño* to qualify for elite cred. The paparazzi have already uncovered my reservation for our late dinner. Let's have a lark as they try to convince their gossip editors that I'm consorting with a woman. Even worse, who they can't identify. Are you game?"

"Game on!"

"Sure?" I hope she confirms "yes".

"Don Miguel, I have secrets too. Before I grew too tall, I was a juvenile professional dancer—ballet. I miss the stage in my constricted corporate life."

That explains her extreme slimness. All the dancers in my set keep their starvation physique, especially the females, and the good ones never lose that obsession. None wear makeup, either, except when performing on stage.

But what is bizarre is the effect she has on strangers. Like a wayward child that even I cannot ignore. Yet her face is plain, without conventional beauty nor even simulated beauty by

Brazil's flesh masters.

She radiates an aliveness in her expression, as if curious and ready to try anything. Perhaps that eagerness is what suggests a child although she clearly is in her early 40's.

We now giggle as our car zigzags along *Calle Juncal* Street at the designer boutiques nestled amongst the mansions. We dash in and out until I strike rapport with the newest *moda* shop.

"She needs something startling for late night dinner here, with some kind of addition, a jacket or cape perhaps, that will make it acceptable in more conservative New York City," I specify.

"Color, Don Miguel?"

"Virginal white. She is slender enough to carry it off. Select something severely proper. Hide a sensual surprise."

The winning outfit is a pencil sheath from neck to satin pumps. From the back Donna is nude until several inches below the top center indent of her cheeks. I don't care what they throw over it for New York City mores. It is a perfect scream for Buenos Aires.

"Do you dare?" I ask.

"With pleasure."

I can see from the sparkle in Donna's hazel eyes, she really will "exceed all expectations", as they say in the board meetings I memorize as a *consultor* consultant supplying information to my private clients. Yes, this dinner tonight will be pure enjoyment, no work for once.

"For breakfast tomorrow, I'll instruct our butler to provide the cache of local papers, and even those international dailies which might have speculated on us."

"What fun."

On the way back to the *Palacio*, I have the car pause for me to pick up my order at the jeweler's.

"Incidentally, my naughty friend, since dinner is at 11:00 pm, shouldn't we have picked up lunch of some sort today?"

"Of course not. Do you plan to get pudgy? I don't."

I am laughing. Once again, we have something, no matter how small and silly, in common.

In my line of work, I sport this splashy outer to camouflage the somber inner. She camouflages with her controlled outer to hide the splashy inner. Splashy camouflage. Camouflage splashy. Opposites? Yet—

CHAPTER 5

THE UNDERSTANDING
Donna Speaking

As we charge again through those spectacular halls to The King Suite, Don Miguel says "Immediately we must nap, but don't tell anyone."

I'm shocked by his assault on my "hands-off" cabinmate rule.

"No." I am not prepared for such a gauche proposition. Shameful.

"Your choice, Madame. *Porteños* store up energy for our second day. Otherwise, we nod off at the first wine."

I don't answer. I feel I am blushing, but this time with embarrassment for my own being so gauche. For misunderstanding.

"Yes, Madame Cabinmate, we *Porteños* people of the port, live twice—the early first day for work, and later, the second for intellect and pleasure." He chides with devouring pique. I look down foolishly.

"Your culture makes you choose work or play. We combine both to fill the only life our God awarded us." He turns his back.

We nap and yes, in separate beds, and I don't tell anyone.

At 10:00 pm, the butler wakes us bringing Don Miguel's evening clothes with his patent leather designer slip-ons so shiny they look like Cinderella's glass slippers. Once more, we shower and dress—for our second day.

Miguel's car whisks us away from the elite *Recoleta* enclave to the *Boho-Chic Palermo SoHo* section.

Don Miguel points out, "This is where our Jorge Luis Borges

grew up. He's a hero for us, trying so hard to promote and define a national culture *Argentinidad.* But it turns out genocide, dictators, raging inflation and poverty prevented all except the *Milonga* Tango to express our identity of who we are."

"Yes, I tried reading his surrealistic essays, but they are hard to understand since I mostly know New York's underbelly street culture. After this experience of Buenos Aires, I'll try reading him again."

The car circles the *Fogón* restaurant—it closes for tourists like all restaurants at 10:30 pm—and stops in the back alley at the brightly lit entrance marked *"Entregas/*Deliveries". A cluster of elegant people are gathered. Paparazzi cameras flash.

The chauffeur stops and opens the door for Don Miguel, who in turn opens my door, again with that exaggerated mock royal bow.

"Walk close in front of me, as if we are a single figure," he instructs.

He pushes me slightly forward. I perform my descending stairs ballet walk, each foot crossing the other.

Don Miguel partners with an exaggerated tango-alpha-male stomp-and-slide routine.

No one can see my nakedness. The crowd parts. Cameras stop flashing.

As we reach the door, Miguel whispers, "Now slowly step to the side without me hiding your nudity and ring that buzzer with style."

With exquisite slowness, I comply. The night explodes with light as cameras flash. I hear clapping for our performance. Obviously, one favorite pastime for *Porteños* is shopping for, then sharing and celebrating, flash-worthy fashion.

The delivery door opens, and the owner pulls us inside, awarding us the prestige of being first to enter.

He guides us to a hand-hewn table next to an open pit of burning logs. The smoke is sweet in my nostrils, permeates everything, even my clothes and hair, but mostly collects at the super-high gray ceiling of this outdoors—indoors. I look at the slabs of raw beef attached to metal spikes thrust into the inferno.

"This is the only restaurant in Buenos Aires that AUTHENTICALLY grills *gaucho* style", the owner says.

I can see it is going to take quite some time to cook the raw meat, even to *jugoso* very rare, and wonder what we will do while we wait.

As more elegant groups enter, I learn. Each table with guests is now graced with attractive male waiters and endless pourings of Argentina's signature Malbec wine. Guests seem to know each other and they visit to chat over glasses of the heady maroon potion.

Ignored, I wish I too were part of this jolly dinner party atmosphere. Amongst my work tasks, "*Traveling Corporate Tech Personal Assistant,*" I've been coached in the rudiments of each of the languages spoken by branches of the conglomerate I work for. In this restaurant, I hear English, Italian, Spanish, French. Even Irish Gaelic my Grandfather Maccoy taught me as the only language he will speak.

As that mid-level computer executive, I choose to be the invisible person accompanying the powers-that-be. But I am miffed that Don Miguel so easily lets me become invisible again. He chooses. Don't I deserve acceptance after I performed so well outside? Or is this my role as well in Argentina, to disappear once the main star comes on stage?

"Don't I deserve acknowledgment from your friends?" I grouch.

"These are not my friends. They are peers."

"So what am I? The ham sandwich?"

"Madame, please observe for yourself what is happening."

I do and see that no "peer" has any incentive to find out who I am. I can be an actress, a whore, any hired stand-in as a partner for this man-about-town. I am attending the party only to satisfy the paparazzi outside.

The real interest is questioning glances, rolling eyes, body tics that can only mean for Don Miguel to spill the beans on what to "peers" is his current off-base public behavior.

I have unwittingly protected *Mister* de Casas. The morning dailies will feature nearly totally naked me, not *Mister*-Collecting-

Nods-of-Respect-Casas.

This isn't innocent. He isn't innocent. He planned it this way to keep his precious respect alive and well—unsullied.

Realizing I have drunk a huge quantity of wine, I excuse myself to the powder room.

When I come out, I pause at the door and look over what amounts to a private midnight restaurant for Argentine elites. Flat-brimmed Spanish *gaucho* hats and horse blankets decorate the walls, where a squadron of male waiters stands at attention.

Oh my God, those six faces look awfully familiar. Those are the same bodyguards who escorted Miguel onto the plane to Buenos Aires. When they sport a waiter uniform and not that bodyguard getup, I can't be sure, but it must be them.

Back at our table, I am treated to slices of *gaucho* grilled beef— *asado.* It is amazing, succulent and juicy with a freshness of the grassy plains, even better than the best steak house in Manhattan can ever offer.

By 3:00 am, it is time to end this "second day."

"Before we leave, I would like to give you a token of our Explore-Day", Don Miguel whispers.

I open the small package he sets before me. It contains a silver money clip and a gold bracelet with a low rectangular box where the clock face would have been if a wristwatch.

This time it is I who look quizzically into his eyes.

"It is traditional for the wealthy to give a discreet gift to a new acquaintance to promote *el acuerdo* The Understanding," he answers but doesn't answer. "A bracelet for you, and money clip for your son Bruce."

I am not clear what he is messaging. He gently clasps the bracelet onto my wrist.

He continues, "I will add your son's initials to his clip, but I need to know if he has a middle name."

"No, just BK." I finger the tiny pendant, the vertical infinity symbol I wear always around my neck, after the attack.

"BK? What about Maccoy?"

"Bruce is my love child."

CHAPTER 6

ARECO RIVER
Miguel Speaking

As my town car drives through the empty streets, I muse about that love child. Is Bruce the husband's problem with the marriage? Donna says her spouse is so elderly he can't – could it be, won't —travel. An affair? Many? Yet something feels odd. She exudes a nervous scent that she doesn't understand why she is attracted to me. By contrast, I know very well why I should not be attracted to her.

In the morning, Donna and I manage to make it to the 8:00 am breakfast announcement. "We have with great effort arranged for an exclusive *Gaucho* Day. You are a lucky group. Most tours are stuck in barren Ushuaia for ship loading and preparation. You will have an exciting day in the *Pampas* grasslands."

I watch breakfasters stare at each other. Are they deciding to be thrilled or angry?

Donna scowls.

I begin to explain the Three-Day-Rule, "If a storm lasts more than a day in the Passage, it's fated to last a week."

"We will be stuck here that long?"

"No, Madame, after the third day we sail no matter what. Otherwise, the tour is refunded. It's in the contract you signed."

I know it's all part of the delay "commission" Buenos Aires exacts from each Antarctica tour. I spout the words of this presumed logic if the tour prospectus has failed to detail the days in Argentina reducing the days in Antarctica.

"Seriously?"

"A modern ship caught in a Drake storm has never sunk, but refunds turn profits into debt. Several tour businesses have sunk that way."

"Hmmph"

"Don't complain, Madame Maccoy. You chose this adventure excursion."

"I'm not complaining. I'm marking territory."

"What?"

"Yesterday, you led the Explore-Day because you know the city's secrets 'intimately' and I've never been here before. It was logical for you to be leader."

"How does that make *Gaucho* Day yours to decide what we do?"

"Because, Sir Casas, I know ranching...intimately."

The tour leader once more interrupts the audience's grousing. "You will find outdoor gear on your luggage racks. We have engaged a private bus to escort you to the *Estancia* ranch—two hours away".

"Donna, give me a "for example", why you propose this is your territory."

"Ever heard of the Maccoy *Fonn Na Saoirse* Ranch in Ireland?"

"Which region?"

"That doesn't matter. Munster if you must know, Miguel. But that's not the point. You don't know anything about cattle, and I do."

I raise my eyebrow at her claim I know nothing of ranching.

She switches tactics. "Besides, it's my turn," daring me to reverse our roles.

"Acknowledged." There is no point in speaking about my experience on the *Pampas*. Any *Porteño* psychoanalyst will detect a manic grab of two weeks' anonymity to break out from her self-imposed restrictions. But her attempt wobbles. Docile and childlike one minute, demanding and prickly the next.

Back in our King Suite, Donna and I replace our "plane-to-Ushuaia" clothes with somber *Pampas* outfits–black eighteenth century style Spanish hat, puffy *bombachas* trousers, wide leather sash-belt, and indigenous poncho.

"Don Miguel, why are we wearing the same outfits?"

I can't help my chuckling. "The tour presumes you American women won't dress like my mothe–," I muddle the word, "like indigenous girls the *gauchos* visit."

"Dress how?" She didn't seem to catch my slip. Indeed, she rattles me.

"Torn rags and a red ribbon, the gift from her renegade lover."

When she is not looking, I take the Glock from the portmanteau and slip it beneath my belt. *Pampas* cannot be trusted. *Porteños* without family still disappear.

Arriving at *San Antonio* village, the tour pauses at the *Museo Gaucho,* followed by required forays into tourist shops.

"It's romanticized, Madame Maccoy."

She glances at the museum cases. "Americans romanticized our outlaw cowboys too."

The sidewalk stall with replicas of the deadly *facónes* knives has a steady business.

"*Gauchos* didn't have guns," I say as I see her study my scar.

I ignore her widened eyes and continue to the next booth. It is doing brisk business selling metal *maté* cups, imitating real gourd cups used by locals, with two sippers for tourists too squeamish to share the single straw.

"*Maté*? Like a cup of bitter green tea, I've heard. I'd rather stick to coffee," Donna says.

"That's not how *maté* is consumed. It's neither a cup of tea nor a coffee replacement. Since I guarantee we again won't make it to Ushuaia tomorrow, I'll treat you then to real *maté*."

When the bus arrives at the private Estancia, the tour leader announces, "You now have 7 hours to do as you please. All facilities and horses are available, an *asado* dinner at 6:00 pm and the bus leaves at 8:00 pm. It's summer—95 degrees Fahrenheit — so don't forget those water bottles. Enjoy your *Gaucho* Day."

"Could I inquire how many acres are fenced?" Donna shouts.

"5800 *hectáreas*," the ranch owner shouts back, "including our *Areco* river."

Donna turns to me. "How big is that in acres?"

"15,000. I don't think we're going to find those fences," I laugh.

She seems excited with that answer. Donna is clearly plotting something for us to do.

Leader or not, I want to be on those horses, so I prompt with a leading question. "Do you ride?"

Her grin doesn't need words to confirm.

We attach water bottles to the small saddles and hoist ourselves onto our steeds. As we forge ahead, the watered green grass surrounding the estate buildings burns brownish in the unwatered meadows under the scorching humid heat.

"Beat you to the river—," she shouts.

That challenge explodes into our wild ride.

I get there first and survey the narrow muddy waterway making its slow drift to the *Río de la Plata* port. I stand by while my horse drinks from the warm river brew.

"They need more than drinking," Donna calls out when she catches up to us. "They need to water down."

She tosses off her clothes, even her bra and panties. Artists' friends model nude and dancers do costume changes backstage —we consider nakedness no big deal. But for me, protected these days by my hard-won public "brand", the habits of a homeless 11-year-old earning *centavos* any way he could, are habits best buried.

"Madame Maccoy, why are you doing that?"

"Giving him a bath to cool off," she calls.

Naked as Lady Godiva, she remounts, and canters into the river, laughing and shouting for me to join her.

I am not about to follow her escapade. I have secrets I don't care to share. "And when someone shows up also searching for the river?" I shout back.

"Won't happen. They just want to eat and drink and pretend they are rich landowners. We're free from all that and can have real fun."

Donna is taunting me.

She doesn't wait for me to decide. She comes dripping out of the river and stomps her foot.

"Weren't you ever a kid, Don Miguel?"

She can't know, but her words are dangerous. They force me to perform like she thinks a kid would react.

I throw off my clothes now and join her in the water. Splashing and chasing each other, riding bareback, diving to grab the other's feet to upend, playing laughing playing.

I know she will see the scar, the slash from my collarbone to belly. "I was an infant," I start to explain.

Now she startles me with the "too dangerous for me to know" signal, a quick snap of the head to the right with follow-up arc of the hand like a salute.

"No?" I question.

She shakes her head "No".

I have no idea where she learned that sign—maybe as a mime dancer. Her message is not to lay bare my secrets, but to merely play with her. Is there anything true about her? Could that husband be a ruse, a faux "hands off"? Those times I caught her blushing...I wonder.

When we have had enough splashing, we climb out of the sultry river. Horses flop on their sides to rest. Separately on each, we lean back on their bellies. If this is what being a kid is like, it is good.

Dozing on the bus back to Buenos Aires, I try to imagine a tall immigrant outlaw father impregnating an indigenous mother to produce me. I can't visualize it.

Skinny Donna, dressed like a man next to me, I can imagine fondling.

CHAPTER 7

PUNISHMENT
Donna Speaking

I am glad to be out of those sweaty clothes. Though we'd spent most of yesterday naked in near 100-degree humidity, the gallop to and later fast canter on those horses returning from the river, ruined those *gaucho* outdoor outfits. Back in our King Suite, after a refreshing bath, then drifting into dreamland in that cool bed by the window, with a satin sheet draped over me, it's Heaven.

By morning, I give up getting to Antarctica and start fluffing and folding the sweaters from my suitcase and putting them in the armoire, where I discover the TV. Where I should have looked when I first checked in. I set the channel to stream the tour's announcements and call our butler to bring a pot of coffee. "Black, thank you."

"Hey *Porteño*—you Buenos Aires port native, claiming every year bedding in this same room, wake up and open those brown eyes. Why didn't you tell me where to find the TV?"

"Did you ask?"

"Oh wow. They're announcing we go to Antarctica tomorrow."

Looking at me he recites, "Prepare your luggage and place it outside your door tonight. We leave for Ushuaia at 6:30 am. Breakfast during the flight south," word for word, as if he memorized it. "Yes, Donna, same words every year I take a tour. The Three-Day-Rule rides again."

"YAY double Yay, plus we don't have to attend another so-called American breakfast to hear announcements." I read to him, "Meet in Lobby at 1:00 pm today for a 'Grand Tango *Cena*.' What's that?"

"Nothing much – *Cena* just means dinner."

I turn back to the screen as "dressy clothes" scrolls off. I'm going to have to drag details out of him—again, "and a Tango *Cena*?"

"Ah, that's something else. It starts with an afternoon program showing dances in each phase of our Tango culture. Nineteenth century bordello aggression play, *"Milonga"*—originally by the Africans here, steps added by immigrant sailors dancing together portside. Twentieth century gentrification of male with female intimacy, renamed the *"Tango"*. Today's simplified ballroom style *"Tango Vals"* with a group lesson for tourists."

"That's why dressy clothes?"

"Naturally. Then street food and wine for a leisurely dinner. Finishing up the *Cena*, an evening performance by our most famous dancers and musicians."

"When should it be over?"

"Every tourist place closes by 10:30 pm."

"Perfect. I want to get a good sleep so I can enjoy Antarctica tomorrow."

"I'm going to sleep on the plane. Care to join me after the *Cena* for a *Milonga* hustle? I'm local so we'll be welcome at places way past the wee hours—you know, our *Porteño* people of the port, culture..."

I ignore this craziness. "For the *Cena*, should I wear my white dress?"

"Absolutely not. *Porteños* have already seen that in the gossip sheets. Toss or save for New York City if you will wear it there."

"There's always those travel-to-Ushuaia clothes," I try to lighten the vibe.

"No," he grouses. "Don't you believe in opportunities to create an entrance?"

That is how we end up pacing the southern Tango barrios for my "dressy" clothes. "Miguel, this reminds me of New York City's Upper West Side, where second-floor rehearsal halls blast music from open windows..."

Here in the muggy chipped-paint barrio, dancers escape steamy studios onto the streets, accompanied by guitarists strumming rapid 2/4 beat practice tunes. Stomp sway stomp cacophony.

Here too passersby nod respect. "Miguel, one of those little street dancers is bowing to you. Why?"

"I used to be a popular professional dancer, but we *Porteños* dance until we die, Madame Maccoy. Not the tourist Tango, but *Milonga* machismo. It takes huge energy and passion—better for health and spirit than your elite fitness facilities."

He shrugs, continuing, "Perhaps some like me still inspire others."

It's a plausible answer but I want more. "So those street dancers tango together but with sailor steps?"

"Brilliant, Madame. Tarantella, Czardas, African, Polka, Flamenco, Gypsy – steps from all the sometime immigrants mishmashed with a generous touch of humor."

"I like that scarlet dress she's wearing. It's my favorite color when I'm not on corporate duty. I'll get a red dress today."

"No, don't you understand? With me, in public, you are on 'corporate duty.'"

"I didn't bargain for that on my 'letting loose' adventure tour."

"Well, that's what you got."

With that finality, I am fitted at the dance suppliers with a slinky black sequin dress slit to the hip on the right and in back to half that height. Open toe stilettos with flexible leather shanks, engineered for partnering on the balls of the feet. I get it that the high heels are there to keep balance as I try out rapid steps and pivots.

It's nice buying new things, but I'm still irritated. I really want a red dress like that street dancer.

"Are we done yet?" I pout. "What's this submission-dominance schtick?"

"My dear Donna, how can you think of such a dastardly deed, my hyper-sensitive consort."

"Well, it feels like you are punishing me for yesterday—my forcing you to play like a kid."

"I don't do punishment."

"Bull, I know punishment. Don't try to brush me off." At least he's paying for the stuff. I'll toss it overboard once we are on that ship.

"Not at all, Madame Cranky. Here's the answer for 'Are we done yet.' You can't go to Tango *Cena* looking like a fence post hanging out in a sexy dress."

"As I said before, *Mister* Casas, I will not get pudgy for you. Or anyone."

"Calm down. Stop your tantrum. We just need to see Madame Gina's fitters."

"For what?"

"The Brazilian bump."

"Miguel, I swear if anyone touches me, I'll call the police."

"Stop stop stop. Use that brain of yours. Understand the mechanics of the butt. There are no muscles in the fat – so even the Brazilian surgery droops over time. Celebs use a specially designed butt shaper undergarment, and because those sailors saved genital friction for the bordello, the *Milonga* is danced with a wide space between the partners' parts there, as the woman–or the man playing a woman–arches her back and pulls her rear away from the man's parts. The shaper emphasizes her now extravagantly rounded butt."

"No knives? No scalpels?"

"Do I have to answer that? Really Donna?"

"No Miguel, I myself choose, on my own, without your help, without your insistence, or anything else, to believe you—this time."

We pound up the stairs to Madame Gina's for an angry fitting where I feel like a naughty child having my mouth washed out with soap. We crash back down to the street where dancers stop and stare at us glowering at each other. He signals his car to pick us up.

From the sidewalk, he throws the purchases into the back and climbs into the seat himself without assisting me. "Satisfied? I can leave you here to fend for yourself. You'll be just another easy target to molest or worse. Let that sink into your trusting wits...

Now get in. I DON'T DO PUNISHMENT."

Back at the *Palacio*, we dress silently and join the group at 1:00 pm on the dot. We ride together but sullen in the cadre of limousines heading to the Tango palace. No way Miguel can even think about making an entrance now that we seem to be crumbling apart.

Still not speaking, I see the program and dinner are ridiculously touristy, not worth the hundreds of dollars the tour pays for each of us, albeit tour members smile plenty—so success.

Square tables with red or blue cloth covers range along the walls, surrounding the wood dance floor where the program and group lesson take place. Some tables have a party of 4; ours is just Miguel and me. We are sitting next to each other, on the viewing side of the table.

If we were talking, I would tell Miguel how much I love the music squeezing out from that *bandoneón* concertina. Those notes slide with a dreamy wistfulness. The mournful tune takes over my brain. I smile.

Dinner is obviously where the palace makes some profit, serving cheap street food, a modest single entrée, and run-of-the-mill Malbec. Though for me, dinner is interesting to see what regular people eat. We are still not talking so I don't need to comment on the first course, *empanadas.* Big deal, every Latin country makes them.

The *maître d'* announces, "For the entrée, please enjoy our 'Argentine Classic *Lomo de Cerdo a la Caucana*' (Milk Pork)." I pick at the curdled milk and simmered meat.

"Donna, you're not even tempted to try the dish?"

I sigh. "Isn't anything authentic here? This isn't an Argentine classic, it's everyday South Italian country food."

"That's the point. '**Argentinidad takes possession of the whole of Western culture, and we have the right to take it**.' If you had read more of our Borges and his saying that, you would understand us better now."

"Giant melting pot?"

"Not at all, Donna. We take 'as-is' our indigenous', slaves', and

immigrants' cultures to mix and match. We like it this way."
He chuckles, "Sometimes there's a happy accident and we invent
something totally new. It's coming up now as dessert."

"*Dulce de Leche* in coffee?"

"Centuries ago, the Argentine ruler's servant forgot to take milk
off the simmer stove, and a day later discovered it had turned into
sweet caramel sticky liquid. It's become our unique classic enjoyed
worldwide today".

The aroma of the smokey coffee with swirls of milk caramel is
delicious. What possesses me to ruin this by whining just when
we're trying to patch up? "My butt shaper feels like a misplaced
throw pillow, Don Miguel. Does anyone notice this getup you
coerced me into?"

"I notice."

Damn, am I so frustrated I can't control this mouth? Getting
attention this way doesn't feel like me – I keep blaming it on
hormones, but... "Don't glare at me," I say, but now quietly.

"Hurt feelings? Time for our *maté*. I do keep promises." Miguel
calls a waiter and gives him a small empty gourd with silver collar
and short metal sipper spoon.

"Where did that come from?"

"*Maté* requires your own gourd. This is mine, from our room."

Good grief. I'd better get back to normal. I missed such an easy
tell. Miguel may be weird, but he is not mean. At least he is trying
to get along, yet I don't seem to even try.

When the gourd is returned with a steaming ripple on the
bitter yellow herbs, Miguel teaches the language. "It's camaraderie
first, but mostly acceptance."

He swirls the spoon and shows me its base has a screen to
keep the loose herbs from the sipper handle. "Now pretend we are
friends who catch up on recent doings over *maté*–like Americans
go to Starbucks for a casual get-together."

"Chit chat chit chat – Now what?"

"Nothing. It takes at least a half hour to cool to sipping
temperature."

"What if you are hungry?"

"Tough."

Some other tables have a *maté* cup and the people seem relaxed and yes, chit-chatting.

Finally, Miguel raises his gourd and takes a sip through the spoon's handle.

"Now if I pass it to you, I am saying I accept you in my set."

"Do you want me?" I look into his eyes.

"Will you accept me back?"

At that moment, I want more than anything to be accepted by this scarred mystery man. To be wanted. Totally wanted.

"Steady there, Donna" He takes my trembling hand and wraps it with tonight's warmth. I am gasping and shaking. I lean down to the spoon handle, swirl my tongue, and slowly lick its length. Finally, I inhale a sip of the bitter liquid. I learn it behaves like caffeine in *Cafecito*, Miami's potent shots of Cuban coffee. The shot of *maté* to my body is swift and exciting.

"Now wait for the jolt to subside," Don Miguel says. "Lovers use this time to tell what they will do with each other later–we can relax and enjoy that you are now accepted in my set."

Fonn. My brain chants that Gaelic word for "desire". It sounds like Frown, but it's Smile I crave for his assent. "Want..." I whisper and beg his eyes.

"Donna, you may ache, but do you dare want me—as I am?"

CHAPTER 8

CRUISING
Miguel Speaking

All I can think in my surreal overly passioned state when I next hear "Don Miguel, how do I accept you?" is truth. This is becoming more than play.

"You have already accepted me," I whisper as I lean closer to Donna's trembling body. "If you had refused to drink, that would have ended us."

"So simple?"

"So simple. If we meet again, we will sip *maté* together to renew our acceptance. That is how *Porteños* create community."

"What you call your set, Don Miguel?"

"Our set."

Turning to the performance, I feel bad for the dancers constricted to the waltz-like *Tango* acceptable to tourists.

"Many of those dancers are members of our set," I tell Donna.

The loudspeaker chimes. "For our finale", the Master of Ceremonies announces, "please welcome Alejandra and Ezequiel, who have just won the Gold Medal in Milan's International Competition."

Tour members politely clap after the couple performs a credible rendition and bows.

"Donna, watch," I whisper to her. "Now the *Porteños* will take over." Sure enough, the two dancers remain in the middle while the local audience vacates their chairs to sit on the floor, clapping and whistling, chanting *Zotto, Zotto, Zotto.*

"*Zotto?*" Donna asks.

"He invented our favorite *Milonga*. No one will go home until someone dances it."

Alejandra circles the floor, slowly doing that pantomime sexual play to each male, yes I feel you, no not so much, maybe the next fellow? Searching for her partner with the familiar Milonga pre-dance heightening of the room's sensual tension, priming it for release. When she comes to our table, she signals with left-turning eyes her invitation to me.

I can signal "No".

I choose to join her. I imagine I am holding Donna as this unexplained passion forces perhaps the best *Zotto* I've ever performed.

"Encore. Encore." I see even Donna call for Encore. The clapping becomes a rhythmic chant, but I need Donna and stride back to our table.

Now the chant turns into Chippy Chippy to insist I return. Ezequiel tactfully replaces me and performs the encore.

"Chippy, Don Miguel?"

"Yes. Sometime, but not now." I remind Donna she has already asked about Mrs. Chippy, the cat.

After this finale encore, both dancers join our table to relax.

"So simple…" Donna repeats, as all four of us share my gourd.

On the return to the hotel, she whispers "I wish that had been me there".

I know she is saying a more sweeping message, that she would have wanted a different life. I'm sure she saw that Alejandra is nearly a head taller than Ezequiel, but relative height doesn't matter to us *Porteños*. Many of our men are short with Sicilian or indigenous ancestors—yet those two dance together and even win prizes. Where you were born is indeed the crapshoot of existence.

Back at the hotel, I ask again, "Donna, this may be our last chance to enjoy Buenos Aires together, so please, join me for *Milonga* cruising tonight."

It excites me when she nods yes.

As we pack our luggage for the overnight transfer to the Ushuaia plane, I give her the small gift I'd picked up for her in the barrio.

"I'm touched that you always wear your *el acuerdo* bracelet. This you should also wear tonight."

I pick up a bag I'd thrown into the car during our dustup and toss it to her. "I'll call my chauffeur while you dress."

Donna peeks into the bag and catches her breath.

Right there, facing me, she unlatches the neck clasp holding up the bodice and lets the black sequin tango dress fall to the floor, revealing her panties and nude form.

From the bag I gave her, she pulls out a red barrio style Tango dress -- elastic top with neck strap to keep the front secure, and swirly slit skirt flaring out from the waist.

"Don't pack your tango shoes, you'll wear them tonight too."

"Thank you", she whispers and twirls around in circles, showing me how alive she feels.

Is that the secret to dealing with Donna? Think of her as the primal child, incorrigible, infuriating, but endearing and yes, lovable?

As we put our luggage outside our door, I explain. "Now you look like a local—your off-rack red slit dress is the favorite with barrio *Porteños* and tonight you'll see the authentic city—no tourists allowed".

She peers outside the lobby. "Miguel, where is your town car?"

"Right here, you're looking at it."

"That flatbed pickup truck with those gangsters?"

"Not gangsters—my posse and yes, some are armed, Donna. Tonight, we will fit in, drop our entitled personas, be our real selves. But, we still must keep our guard up in places we will frequent."

I see her take in this dented "barrio town car" wreck of a flatbed pickup, with bodyguards lounging in the truck bed. Three of us fit in the front seat, chauffeur, Donna and me.

"Sorry Donna, I need to be on the inside, the protected seat–why don't you switch with the guys in the shotgun lounge, so one of them can sit window."

"No, Miguel, that's sporting of you, but I'll take my chances. You dared me to desire you as you are. Don't stop me."

We peel out, with me between the expendable driver and "don't stop me" stubbornly expendable Donna.

As usual, the posse knows where the aficionados of the social *Milongas* are headed tonight – mass get-togethers for overnight dancing – no food, no alcohol, no drugs – just live volunteer musicians or YouTube recordings–huge empty, often abandoned, second floor rooms, no furniture since everyone sits on the floor around the perimeter to clap and stomp the rhythm. Whoever wants to dance, invites a partner to shuffle, spin, and step counter clockwise around the floor for several rounds of tunes, then can pick a new partner and start all over again.

I teach Donna the movements of the *Zotto*, and she giggles at the high kick she performs—carefully enough—between my splayed legs. Soon we are clapped into the middle of the floor and perform this favorite *Milonga* for all to stomp and enjoy.

Tonight, my team gets to relax without work assignments and except for my chauffeur, who stays in the truck secure with his own Glock (he sleeps with it), the other six members wander about–sometimes *Milonga* dancing together in gay pairs.

"Fewer people hate here anymore, Donna. We're proud to be so accepting -- did you know Argentina was the first on this continent to enable same sex marriage and our nature leans toward individuality and unabashed open mindedness, in everything -- even our Jesuit Pope Francis was considered by some conservatives outside of Argentina, too liberal to be elected Pope. Though there's always room to grow, we are proud to have progressed from some of the excesses of last century's violence into today's more tolerant refuge for all."

"I love that," she whispers as we dance, but straightens her back, collapsing the safe space between our genitals. Is she trying to embrace me? I shudder and politely finesse her return to the *Milonga* no-touch posture. I hope she doesn't notice I'm turned off–or scared?

Next morning, tour personnel get us all on the plane to Ushuaia, that forlorn penal colony named "Argentina's Siberia" on the southern tip of Latin America.

"Donna, I've already arranged for you to join me in the seat next to me." Separated by our seatbelts, we lean toward each other and sleep through first class service—*QED*, a cashmere blanket—for the next four-hours.

"Welcome to Port Ushuaia, the official port for Antarctica tours" our chatty tour leader announces. "You have 30 minutes at leisure while we load Swan Hellenic's Vega. If you check out the historic radial Prison, wear a sweater as this far south, summer is not 95 degrees but more like 50. Most important, take your anti-seasickness pills now as they don't kick in for an hour."

"Nonsense," Diana huffs and flounces her red barrio *Milonga* dress. "I never get seasick. I'd rather take a quick hike to those gorgeous mountains so close to us here."

"Have you ever cruised the Drake Passage?"

"OK, to make you happy, I'll pick up some Dramamine at that tourist shop over there." She takes off her Tango stilettos and walks barefoot to it.

I join her there. The shop is the only shop in the Port that caters to Antarctica tourists who forgot to pack essentials like toothpaste or breath mints. I know the clerk from the many times I have killed time here, chatting about Tierra del Fuego weather, local gossip, Buenos Aires gossip, anything spicy and entertaining. It keeps me on her good side and we've become fond of each other.

Donna comes up to the register with a small packet of Dramamine.

"I suggest, Donna, you go back and get the big 36-count box."

After she leaves, I pre-pay and hand a packet of American dollars to the clerk. We grin at each other, Argentine problem-solvers at heart.

Donna returns. "Don Miguel, I'm ready to pay."

"No time, Donna, they've announced the ship boarding. I took care of it."

"You didn't have to."

I am tired of these puerile arguments and shrug.

"No time left either, Donna, to hike those Tierra del Fuego mountains over there."

ANNALONZO

We turn to board the huge ship.

CHAPTER 9

BEHOLD
Donna Speaking

Just like on the streets of Buenos Aires, where Miguel is recognized with nods of respect—and even a bow from that little street dancer—on the wide gangplank to the 4th Deck Reception area, Swan Hellenic's Vega ship staff seem rushing to make sure he is fully welcomed and profusely greeted.

"Miguel, have you already been on this ship? It's new, says the tour guide."

"No, never."

The head of reception dashes to our place at the check-in desk and loudly and quite publicly announces, "Don Miguel de Casas, we are so honored," and gives a showy nod of respect, almost a short bow.

I notice all his assistants stop and peer at this celebrity passenger too.

"And Miss Maccoy, welcome."

"Madame," Miguel corrects him.

"*Pardonnez-moi, mon erreur,* Pardon me, my error, Madame Maccoy."

I'm about to do the polite global nod of appreciation for the correction when Miguel keeps going.

"My colleague." I stare at him for telling this fib, though I quickly recover and now make the polite global nod.

I guess he has his reasons, but I have my reason not to be connected publicly with this strange *Porteño*. The company where I work has branch offices, in fact the Argentine address is near

Recoleta, and it's only a matter of time when I'll be assisting a Board Member or high executive to review in person the Latin American branches. The last thing I need on those trips is being recognized or worse, being greeted by name. My whole strategy at the conglomerate is to be invisible, enabling my bosses to be the only stars. I'll definitely discuss this privately with Miguel.

Meanwhile we are grandly escorted by a selected personal steward from the group waiting for assignments, onto the lift elevator to the 6th Deck. The steward even leads us to the door to our cabin, offering to check if everything is *comme il faut* as it should be, inside.

I'm curious how Miguel carries himself with this attractive young steward.

"No need, sir." I see him discreetly take a folded $50 US dollar bill from his pocket and slip it to him even though tips are included in the tour price. Our steward is pleased. Not demeaned by the usual attitude toward what are essentially ship servants. The precious American dollars don't do that either, but "sir" acknowledges him as the man he should be. So simple. I wish everyone could show such spot-on empathy.

Miguel now unlocks the door and treats me to his usual mock royal bow, waving me in to enter first.

"Oh my God, Miguel. This Pemium Suite is AMAZING". There's a wall of floor to ceiling windows, overlooking a now more active sea, sculpted by a mottled gray sky where soaring seabirds struggle against what must be gusts of wind. I look out onto the prow of the ship where there's that monumental, tall black archway the brochure calls "The Swan's Nest" observation post.

This first room has a gigantic California King Size bed parallel to the window wall. Between the bed and the windows is a square accent table, a bit large, metal with rounded corners, and designed with a modern single pedestal—it's securely bolted down when I try to move it closer to the sofa perpendicular to the windows. I check the adjoining room—a living room with an electric fireplace and now go looking for the second bedroom. I go back to the front bedroom and check its door—to a large fancy en suite walk-in closet, dressing room and separate bathroom, filled with luxurious lotions and scents.

"Miguel, granted this huge suite is at least the size of half a football field, but did you know there would be only one bed?"

"Of course not. I'm here learning. So Americans will compare this size of the Premium Suite to a football field? How quaint. I expect it to serve as a Bridal Suite, and if no wedding, the Presidential Suite with staff housed in the smaller more affordable cabins on the lower decks. That's where we'll be housed on the return trip."

"Why?"

"So my assessment will be all-encompassing."

"You sound like a Mystery Reviewer. Are you?"

"*Consultor* consultant, Donna. I don't write reports – have you ever seen me write anything? No, I sip *maté* with our Minister of Tourism, as his dear friend and confidant. Remember how I showed you how we create community with *maté*."

There's a knock on the door. It's our personal steward.

"Don Miguel, emergency training will take place in 15 minutes at the Base Camp on Deck 3. Would you like me to escort you and your colleague now?"

"No, we need to dress first. But when we leave, if you would sort out our clothes, I would appreciate."

I always wear my silver infinity necklace and the gold *acuerdo* bracelet, which don't go together normally, but I embrace this marriage of mixed metals. These symbols belong together.

I find my comfy Crocs Kadee flats and am able now to climb off the Milonga stilettos.

I consider next what is in my suitcase—sweaters, slacks and those fancy evening clothes from Buenos Aires, and ask, "Miguel, I think I'm going to still wear the red dress you gave me, if you don't mind. It is a special gift. Okay?"

Miguel answers me with something so unexpected. This former dancer silently motions me to watch him dress. Inside the walk-in closet, posing for my eyes only, he draws out of his wardrobe trunk an intricate jumpsuit, something Versace could have designed, black faille with ebony silk ribbons streaming at shoulders, elbows and wrists. Striking attitudes, he slowly disrobes and hangs his tailored dark suit outfit, reaching a pose high toward the ceiling, then seductively twists to select a pair of black velvet Medusa slip-ons for his shoes. I'm mesmerized as he slowly steps into the jumpsuit. His body is a thing of beauty, how it moves and halts, proportioned like those slender male dancers in Madonna's Vogue performance. The silk ribbons reflect movement as he gestures, as if alive too. I'm stunned, captured by his performance. Too soon it ends; Miguel is dressed. Back to the real world, I wonder who would guess beneath the provocative black silk lies a scar so long and white against his brown-toned chest, it's a wonder he survived whatever carved it.

We make it down to the 3rd Deck Base Camp and sit cross-legged on the floor with the rest of the tourist group. It feels like a party. Or like we are a cub scout pack, eager to follow our leader. Or happy *Porteño* dancers at a *Milonga* fest, ready to clap and stomp for whichever of us takes over the dance floor.

Don Miguel seems sincerely interested in sea lore. "In the old days, Donna, before the little Lindblad Explorer sank, this would have been painted white with red letters attached: "Muster Station". No sea people back then needed instruction to assemble at it for possible rescue in an emergency. Today thousands of enthusiastic tourists, not seasoned expedition explorers, swarm over 30 huge Antarctica cruise ships, resulting in strict safety regulations. We'll be treated to how to get into the zodiacs, kayaks, and even the covered lifeboats 'for access to the mainland'. But it's surrogate regulation compliance – we can't leave port until everyone has heard these safety measures."

While all this is going on, I hear the winds rising outside the boat. even though we are still in port. As we leave the safety training, the ship makes its way into the Drake Passage, 620 miles of choppy sea dreaded by sailors of yore—and I daresay some crewmates and tourists even with today's advanced safety technology.

Back up at our 6th Deck cabin, the balcony area has gotten quite windy under a now tempestuous angry sky. Miguel greets our steward with a question – "Is the Bridge still open for visitors?"

"Yes, Don Miguel. But I hear scuttle it will be closed shortly. So, if you want to visit, you'd better climb up quickly." We go our separate ways.

Miguel grabs my arm and says "Run. Something's up." We take the lift to the 7th Deck and even though the ship is now rocking and no longer level and stable, we climb the stairs to the highest point on the ship, the walls of high-impact windows, the captain's Bridge. Winds are swirling madly, the back of the Bridge is still open and Miguel practically shoves me inside.

The Captain is conferring with the tour leader, explaining how this sudden storm is blowing in from the West but we will navigate through it. Miguel interrupts. "How low is the pressure?" and I don't catch nor understand the numbers and words they exclaim to each other.

"How long?" The leader asks.

"Quarter hour, cabins fore and aft on the ship will feel the swells buffet them. The mid-ship cabins maybe half an hour, but their windows will already dull with wave spume."

Miguel now speaks directly to the Captain "Please know that I was on the Explorer when it sank in 2007 and I have skills no one would imagine. I helped tether together the escape rafts and nearly drowned keeping people alive, waiting to be noticed by any passing freighter back then. So, if you need any help, ANY EFFORT, when this storm hits with force, please know I'm just downstairs in the Premium Suite and can be available to you."

Now he turns to the tour leader, "My colleague here is not a seaman, but as a dancer, she harbors reserves of energy and determination that you can call on if inside passengers need assistance. Right, Donna?"

I'm shaking now but nod a clear "yes". Not able to think of anything more appropriate, I give the thumbs up sign. I'm hoping Miguel is just following Black Swan protocol—inventorying solutions for work teams with diverse and actionable skills.

"Skills inventory? Miguel? I hope."

"Of course. These huge ships, with emergency stabilizer arms leveling the hulls, don't sink anymore and captains have learned how to go off course to avoid side crashes from storms, but cabin and deck windows can still break and water slamming inside creates mayhem with panicky passengers. Why do you think the Bridge is high-impact resistant glass?"

Miguel continues, "I'll meet you in the cabin shortly. And don't be stubborn. Take that Dramamine."

I climb back down to retreat alone to our cabin.

On our deck, I pause and turn to look one last time at the arch on the prow. There is Miguel standing tall inside the ebony curve, black silks flying with the powerful wind, leaning forward into the maelstrom.

Unforeseen. Disturbing. Untamed.

Behold, The Black Swan.

CHAPTER 10

TAMED
Miguel Speaking

When I return from the Swan's Nest lookout, Donna is standing by the window and faces me with a far-away dreamy expression.

"I saw a mauled bird rising to challenge the sky, Miguel..."

She's approaching the truth. In these moments of ecstasy, I transport to when I was the charge of the Jesuits, reaching for closeness to God in Heaven while trapped in the sticky mass of imperfect. But I can't expose this rapture. I descend to earth.

"Donna, if you only knew," I sigh.

I put my arm around her shoulder and guide her to the sofa by the windows.

"Donna, before we are affected by the swells, we should sit here and plan this thing out."

"Swells?"

"Without a storm, waves are barely three feet high, and then we call it the 'Drake Lake'. Even so, in the dining room, things like place mats and cutlery are taped down because those constant little waves rock this ship like a baby's cradle."

"And with a storm?"

"Waves swell first to 30, then plateau at 65 feet high – that's nearly 6 building stories—spiking at times to 95 feet–8 stories. That's why the captain guides the ship straight up and over the swells to avoid them hitting the side of the boat and threatening the stabilizers, those arms that come out like levelers in the water around the ship's hull."

"Are storms always this dangerous, Don Miguel?"

"The bigger ones are, but climate change makes even smaller ones hard to predict. What's constant is the up and down zig-zag, where the down is practically like slamming the ship into the low point toward the sea bed. There are even loud noises, like explosions, but not real explosions. Going over each swell, it's the crash, the slam-down of the hull and the vibration that shake the outer structures and the air around us."

"Good grief, Miguel."

"That's why we need, Donna, to stay put next to something we can grab onto. Take that table over there. It's bolted to the floor and the slender pedestal is easy to hang onto."

"Are you seriously suggesting we crouch under that little table until the storm is over? How long is that?"

"In concept, under the table, yes. Because there are no landmasses to break up this whirlpool of ocean around Antarctica, once you are in a storm you can't escape it - you just have to ride it out until it runs out of energy and stops stirring things up. With luck, 2 days to where we're headed, though 3, 4 or even 5 days have been known."

"Miguel, this is insane. Why isn't there an airport to fly into Antarctica and skip this whole ship thing?"

"Ecology Donna. The 50 Treaty holders won't allow what would be disastrous—and irreversible—damage to the continent. Chile has let an occasional extremely expensive charter group land in their South Shetland King George Island, to be met by an exclusive expedition ship this side of the Drake—but it's risky, almost a walk-back to the early experimental Lindblad Explorer days nearly a century ago when everything was chancy, unpredictable, and seriously dangerous."

"Is it really undamaged ecology?"

"Except for maybe mild damage where the tourists hang out, Donna, yes. Even the research stations collect their waste and ship it back to their countries for disposal. They behave as if they are living in space stations—in the last place on earth where it actually is unspoiled."

"I've heard enough, Miguel. It's important for sustainability, but this storm is what concerns me now."

"We've got to do one thing, though, while we can still safely move about. Besides crouching under the table, or leaning over the tabletop to hold onto, we'll need to sleep. Help me gather the seat cushions from both of the sofas in this suite."

I make a narrow floor mattress next to the pedestal for when we sleep.

"We'll have to spell each other. Protect one another. So Donna, when you sleep, I'll hold you from rolling off the cushions, and when I sleep, you should do the same for me."

We use the bathroom one last time and brace for the storm.

As we huddle together, I feel the boat tilt. "Table time, Madame Maccoy—"

For the next 47 hours and 604 miles, Donna dry-heaves—Dramamine can't do miracles.

The cracks set up a regular rhythm as wave after wave assaults this ship. I quickly get used to it, but she seems haunted by some crashing noise in her past. And the secondary clap from jamming every so often into patch ice carried inside the wave, seems to perturb her even more. She's distressed when awake.

When she sleeps and I hold her from rolling, she's not even here on this makeshift cushion-bed. She's somewhere else, being attacked. She keeps whispering "No!!!!!" over and over, receding till it's barely audible. Yet her body itself acts independently from that tortured brain. Her slender form presses into mine and breathes with a quickening heartbeat.

When we're both awake, we try to comfort each other but quickly run out of small talk.

We need action and activity. We can't even dance the *Milonga* with the floor tipping all over the place.

Finally, like amateur contortionists, we challenge each other who can do the most bizarre way to hang onto the edge of the table. We try to out-do each other in form and style, giggling when a boat lurch turns a careening pose into a mad scramble back to the table edge.

"Miguel, if you ever come to New York, with my connection to the performance circles, I think I can connect you to important people."

Well, that's a surprise. So Donna does, or maybe did, have a different life in New York than I'd imagined for her.

Meanwhile, while I was protecting her fitful sleep, I and my sorry brain plot how to manipulate our five days on Antarctica to make up for this dismal sea-passage experience.

The Passage finally calms.

"Don Miguel?" She awakens from her demons into this brightening forever daylight of January.

"Drink, drink!" I hand her a water bottle from the cabin's supply and watch her start the recovery.

Then I continue, "Madame, while I was awake, protecting you in your sleep, I remembered a secret that will bring you much joy."

"Yes?"

"Last time I was in a Drake storm like this one, tamed by today's capable luxury liners, the tour members were so exhausted—mostly mentally, somewhat physically—that they wanted to just step foot on the continent that first day. Then they would retire to the lounge and relax with spa massages and libations for the rest of the trip, having on that first day, checked off another country on their countries list."

"That's your secret?"

"The Adélie penguins are friendly and like to greet people when they come ashore, especially with fun performers like us. You and I can improvise a mime to entertain everyone and put tour members in a good mood after this rough start. We can pose them with the penguins for pictures and members can text to their grandchildren how wonderful is this trip, pictures attached. Then members can retire "successful trip accomplished" to the lounge to relax while we have the continent to ourselves for the next four days."

"Don Miguel, what makes you think tour security will allow us alone on the Ice?"

"I entitle myself."

Donna giggles, "Besides, I bet they don't tell anyone."

Turning quiet, she again projects that dreamy expression from when I entered our cabin from the Swan's Nest observation arch. She starts to say something. Stops. Finally asks, "Have you ever played the game 'Secrets'?"

"No, what is it?"

"It's run by the leader who suggests playing the game," she explains. "There are usually a few days, like a long weekend Airbnb sharing or off-site business conference, where a few people are staying together in one place. Each morning the leader decides and announces a topic. Then throughout the day players think of two stories to tell of how they have a secret about the topic— but only one of their stories is true. After dinner, each tells their stories. At the end of the number of days playing, everyone votes on which in each pair of stories is true. It's a lot of fun and a great way to become acquainted."

"Sounds complicated. Not direct like *el acuerdo,* The Understanding, when I gifted your bracelet."

"Please Miguel–I never imagined keeping in touch with my cabinmate after a tour. But with you it's different. Maybe. I think sometimes I know you enough to want to be friends. But I don't really know you, do I? And maybe you don't want to be friends, even though you've been so generous to me and my son."

I take her hand—it is as ice cold as mine—and look into her eyes. Again, I experience that unnatural attraction I should not be feeling.

"Besides, Miguel, we'll be together for only a few more days. How can it hurt?"

"All right, Donna. I'll play Secrets with you if you agree to this. You can be leader and decide the topics for the first four days, if I can be leader on the fifth, our last day on Antarctica."

CHAPTER 11

DECEPTION
Donna Speaking

The winding down of the Passage crossing can't be more delightful. The Vega stays unmoving with its new technology eliminating an actual anchor damaging the ecology of the sea floor. Here we are, a city block's length away from the shoreline. The windows reveal ice tipped mountains, submerged icebergs, dinner-plate-size ice floaters, and even some penguins off in the distance. But it also reveals a varied dirty white and black shoreline and black mountain bases.

"Miguel, why isn't it all ice? All the gorgeous crystal blues are floating in the sea. I don't see any pristine glaciers on land."

"We're not on **the Ice**. We're on Argentina's tundra here, the duck beak. Look at the map they left in the writing desk in our living room. Our part of the Ice itself is a wide pie slice wedge from the chin of the beak to a point near the South Pole. But this tamer piece of Antarctica, the beak itself, we often get to promote as the real thing. On the map it is officially named "Antarctic Peninsula", so it's got at least Antarctica included in its name. Our tenuous monopoly on the tour industry allows us to avoid wider exploration on the Ice itself. Tourists go along with the switch – the beak meets their expectations in any case."

"Well it's not my expectation. What's this tundra doing here— enlighten this naive tourist, Sir."

"The beak is the same mountain range you saw in Tierra del Fuego—just part of it is submerged by the Drake Passage. Tundra climate is permanently frozen below the surface, but air temperature, though minus-40 degrees in winter, varies from 40 to 50 warm degrees in our summer (your winter up north) – so the winter's new surface ice built in June and July here largely melts in December and January. You tourists can explore here in balmy 50-degree weather. Even so, there's still enough ice left that doesn't melt, though **the Ice** is hundreds of miles away..."

"It sounds like a cheat to me."

"No, just being prudent as tour providers – tomorrow you may see some of the novice actions these tourists make, but we keep close enough control that there have been no deaths–so far."

"Stop saying the Ice. Here is not the real thing."

"Agreed. But it really IS Antarctica."

"Purportedly Argentina keeps going under the Drake Passage to the South Pole?"

"Precisely. Naturally we claim Antarctica.

"Hrpmh"

"Can I tell you something funny to cheer you up?"

"Hrpmh"

"Guess where Argentina laid claim to Antarctica."

"Some dictator claimed it in the Presidential Palace?"

"Funnier than that. Now that you know what our *Argentinidad* character epitomizes—we planted the flag to claim Antarctica on —Deception Island."

"That's so not funny, Miguel, please don't mention it again."

"Agreed. I'm truly sorry you're disappointed. But like Buenos Aires, there are two cultures here – the tourist veneer and the real one I can share with you. I promise."

I feel like I've escaped my stressed New York life to turn up now in a confounding magic realism novel. Not what I thought this 5-star tour was going to be. After all this expense and my gullibility, I'll give this 2-week vacation just one more try—you've got one last chance, elite Antarctica Tundra Tour—I'm certainly never going to trust you again."

"In 15 minutes, please join us in the dining room for supper and celebratory champagne before tomorrow's first day on Antarctica," the intercom announces.

After the champagne toasts, it seems this is a quick tidying up opportunity after the storm is reliably over, as we return to a freshly made bed, sofa cushions back where they belong, and even the wall clock set thoughtfully—instead of Dubai time, the standard for the whole continent apparently, it is set to midway between New York City and Buenos Aires time to lessen jet lag for the elite tour passengers on this cruise.

Next morning, at breakfast—for us, just black coffee as always —the leader instructs the ground rules for landing: "Any time you leave this ship, you must wear your red jacket with correct name ID. Consider it the law down here. You must not discard anything on land—no matter how small or innocuous. Bring your pee jar in case you can't hold it till we return to the ship. Consider it a felony to deposit anything, to disturb anything, and especially not to pick up or take anything. There are no first-time warnings—once caught you will be removed from this tour to resolve your own problem."

"Seriously, Don Miguel?"

"Seriously. The Treaty signers aren't thrilled with tourism here. They feel even the research stations are a threat to this least disturbed ecology on our ravaged planet."

"So why are we allowed here?"

"Market demand, Donna. Too many elite travelers were bored with African photo safaris, after laws enabling shooting the wild beasts were revoked. Antarctica was a suitably costly substitute invented by the exotic tour industry. Argentina jumped right in and made it our own. Annual visitor counts are strictly limited, and at any time, only a small number of tourists can be out on land, usually for little more than an hour. Large tourist ships aren't even allowed to drop anchor near the shore, so many partying younger athletic tourists just take a quick video-photographed dive into the sea so they can record they swam at Antarctica."

The instructor drones on. "Before you enter or leave the Zodiacs that transport you to the Ice, you will suffer inspections worthy of the most thorough TSA perfectionists. This is the warning we will repeat many times: follow the rules."

"So Miguel, once again you make no sense. You said you come here every year for a break to unwind, but this sounds like coming to a gulag."

"Actually, I'm so safe here I don't even bring my protection squad."

"Those bruisers who shadow you everywhere else?"

"Observant, you. And I hear you don't spread around what you figure out. Good."

"That's how I keep my job and pay the bills, as we head-down closed-mouth workhorses guarantee our employers and overseers."

"Appreciated. We all need to survive. And that Secrets game of yours?"

"Before we go down to our suite to dress for our day on Antarctica, I announce the topic for tonight's stories—*Was there any problem with your birth or early childhood?*"

"You'll need to tell your two stories first, so I see how the game is played."

"No problem."

"One more thing, can you improvise a mime with me on the ice today?"

"Try me."

CHAPTER 12

DAY 1 SECRETS
Miguel Speaking

I can never speak too highly of the Zodiacs which ferry us back and forth from ship to land. "Donna, the Treaty specifies only 100 can be on land at a time, so with all of us tourists and necessary crew–one to run the motor and rudder, the other to sort out any passenger issues, and one tour guide who remains on land and supervises the group—they'll use all ten Zodiacs today, creating shifts to whale watch and shifts to explore the land. So don't put on your crampons yet, wait till you climb out onto land."

"Any other advice, while you are in this expansive mood?"

"We'll wait till the last one – the ship has a ladder and a crew member in the Zodiac to hold your hand while you step over the balloon side and onto the hard floor. With the other hand, carry your hiking poles, crampons and pee jar. Once you're on board, put that stuff on the floor next to you."

"Once we're in, then what?"

"Sit on the balloon side, roughly distributing your and everyone's weight equally around the sitting edge and hold tight to the safety ropes—all those 3 foot swells make for a bouncy trip —fun if you are up to it, but terrifying for some folks."

"Why do we want to be on the last Zodiac?"

"Simple math—there will be only a few tourists in the last one —us plus another couple or two. It's more fun to be able to look 360 degrees without having a full boat of tourists crowding the view space. Of course—"

"Of course, what?"

"Human nature being what it is, sometimes the least capable also delay to the last boat—physically unsteady, a bit overweight, elderly not quite up to the challenge—but I volunteer us to help, if needed, to get such hazards safely to and fro...you don't mind, do you?"

"Course not. You have no idea how many times I've helped my boss get a client safely back into their hotel room, and 'forget about it' when greeting the next day. It's a skill—maybe an art —to persuade such clients to believe they've never embarrassed themselves in public. To make sure they dis-remember..."

"Donna, you are full of surprise abilities – how did I not see them before?"

"I was too cautious to trust you—or myself. And I thought your being an elite, you knew all this business tactics stuff already to keep your high status intact."

"Touché. I think our accidental cabinmate meeting that first night—not to speak of my being stood up by my usual cabinmate —caused a disruptive atmosphere. Perhaps under time pressure —we've got only 5 days left together—we are trying to create a different energy going forward?"

"Don't count on going forward. Let's just see what the Secrets game does for us."

We watch the first Zodiacs land their tourists and turn around to return empty to the ship. Ours has two heavyset tour members, so Donna and I make new pairs with ourselves—chubby plus skinny, each pair seated on either side of the boat so it's not dangerously lopsided. *Is this a foreboding that Donna and I are fated to split up to survive?*

Donna climbs out on land first, sloshing in the water as she jumps down. I hear the woman cry out "Oh. So far," and I smell trouble.

"I'll help you Madame," and take her hand to steady her on the swaying Zodiac.

She whimpers, "I'm afraid" and then sits down legs extended in the middle of the boat.

Donna calls out to her, "It's not that far, my cabinmate will help you over the side and I'll be down here to steady you."

The woman now lies flat on her back and refuses to move. I've seen this before, panic attack when nothing is stable underfoot, it can't be helped now. The crew support assistant will suggest the couple return to the Vega—usually the ship crew will need to hoist her up in their emergency harness as she will be in no condition to climb the ladder herself. That really would be dangerous. Oh well, such are tourists who really shouldn't be pursuing this sort of physically demanding adventure. I better jump down now and join Donna while I can.

Now I slosh up to the beach, "I see you've already met some friends, Donna."

"How do you like my waddle, Sir?" she giggles as she imitates the three Adélies who surround her.

"You got it right—you know they physically can't close their arms to their body. They've evolved with strong swimming muscles and tendons starting in the semi-open position so they can hope to escape hungry orcas chasing them in the sea."

We join the other humans and a dozen or so penguins on the top of an icy slope angled toward the water's edge.

"Look, Miguel, they've made a game of sliding down the ice on their bellies, splashing and then waddling to the top and doing it all over again."

"Now if it were a *Milonga* floor, Donna, they'd be like the counterclockwise dancers—let's put on a funny Penguin Tango performance for the tour members."

We find a level spot on the shore and start an exaggerated *Milonga* stomp in a circle counterclockwise, and as the curious birds start to waddle after us, we feel like triumphant Pied Piper wannabe's. Tour members clap from their height on the slope, and everyone has a good time.

"Photo time" shouts the tour guide, as she shepherds them slowly down the slope, showing how to use the hiking poles for stability in the icy slope down route. It's easier to climb up than to go down.

The Adélies enjoy this tour party as much as the members,

and the leader snaps pictures with and without penguins, for distribution before the tour ends.

Success. I overhear couples already telling each other they've seen enough, let's just enjoy the lounge. Massages and latest hit movie projections save a lot of crew energy, and everyone breathes a metaphorical sigh of relief. Happy tourists to spread tour recommendations amongst their well-heeled friends when they return home, are crucial.

After dinner, I leave Donna to give the Captain and tour leader the schedule of when we require the Zodiac to drop us off and pick us back up, since just as I predicted, we will be the only couple still willing to explore on this expedition.

"Donna, it's all set, we have Antarctica to ourselves for the next 4 days."

"Seriously?"

"Of course. When I promise you something, you can count on it. Now let's get on with that Secrets game of yours. You have the floor."

DAY ONE. Donna Story 1: I Was Born a Drugged Fetus.

For six of the nine months I grew inside my mother, she flooded me with illegal diethylstilbestrol—DES, hoping to prevent a miscarriage while I worked at escaping from her not even 3 months into my being —I was too eager for adventure even then. So apart from drugging me into submission, what else did it do? Made cancer drool to ravish my female parts and triggered early menopause—no condoms needed now for a man to ravish me. The End.

"OK, Donna. I'm not sure that's unbelievable, but let's hear your second story."

DAY ONE. Donna Story 2: I Was an Abandoned Infant.

After birth, I was stashed in a Buckminster Fuller Kiddee Koop borrowed from the local orphanage, so my drug addicted mom could ignore me except for occasional feeding and cleaning. When I grew too big for the cage, I was let loose on the floor. This was great because I could teach myself to pull up, then walk and climb, to explore. Figure things out and do anything I wanted. I discovered a world outside. To be safe, I avoided people and learned how to "hide in plain sight." Years later I came back and donated one of those cribs to the Smithsonian American History Museum. You can see it today in the Adirondacks' Great Camps display–it looks like a cream painted rabbit hutch on legs. The End

"Madame Maccoy, I'm skeptical. If I go there, will I see your donation on display? This also sounds too easy to decide it's the false story."

"Nevertheless, you're still going to have to choose which one is true when we are all done. Let's hear if you can do better."

DAY ONE. Miguel Story 1: Cook Did Not Spit-Roast Newborn Me.

There have been facónes knife skirmishes about who controls land in our Patagonian Pampas for centuries. Poverty and revenge instituted cannibalism as the reward for the winning gang or tribe. Most of the eaten are already dead or quickly finished off, like the tribe I was born into. Because I was lengthy for a newborn, the winning gang thought I might grow tall enough to eventually add me to their posse. They brought me to the mission nuns to heal the gashes. I grew into the nuns' child messenger, carrying their letters in my head to mission nuns throughout the region. So I was never cooked and eaten. The End

"A good try, Don Miguel, but Patagonian cannibalism is well known. Your investigative journalists are even today finding new details – I saw the story in the complimentary newspaper at the front desk back at the *Palacio* in Buenos Aires. Try to make your second story better."

DAY ONE. Miguel Story 2: I Was Sold for a Ream of Paper.

The Jesuit Provincial heard rumors of a mystical child delivering messages in the Pampas being prayed to here in the barrios. To destroy this blasphemy, Padre Marcelo was sent to bring back this child to demonstrate an ordinary human being. He found 6-year-

old me delivering messages amongst the missions. The nuns who fed and clothed me said they were too poor to buy paper, and since I remembered and could repeat their words perfectly multiple times, they could not give me to the Padre. "I will trade you a ream of paper for the boy, that's 500 sheets, more than enough to carry your messages on paper." That is how I was sold and taken away from the nuns. The End

"Now you are getting the hang of it, Don Miguel. That does sound unbelievable."

Thinking about tomorrow, it's time for another leading question from me. "Donna, do you dive?"

CHAPTER 13

DAY 2 SECRETS
Donna Speaking

Miguel rummages in his portmanteau trunk and comes up with a black cloth bag.

"Here, Donna, let's see if this fits you." He pulls out two free-dive masks.

"Geez. Gucci?" I check out the monogram.

"I had my jeweler put the monogram on either side so I could keep straight whose was whose."

"Your son's looks a little smaller—let me try that first." Miguel looks startled but hands me the smaller mask.

"Perfect fit. Did you toothpaste off the film on the facemask glass yet?"

"Of course, I always do that early now." He chuckles, "That's how I discovered that Ushuaia shop—my first time here, I was one of those Antarctica tourists who forgot the right toothpaste."

I peer into the bag and see only long 29-degree Italian fins for deep dives, underwater flashlights, and extra batteries on top of a fold of black cloth on the bottom. "Where are the snorkels?"

"Water too cold. Just slightly above freezing. We need to do quick free dives and recover, over and over."

"Okay, Miguel. I'm wondering if you don't actually come here for fun and relaxation—is there always some secret project or on-call service up your sleeve? That you are somehow connected with powers that be, even if loosely. So please trust me—what are we diving to find?"

"Not on board with electronic ears. After we hike alone to the dive locations I'll explain. Meanwhile, let's turn in. The Zodiac brings us early tomorrow."

Next morning, at 6:00 am, I announce the topic for tonight's stories—*What is your special skill or talent?*"

After the Zodiac drops us off and leaves to return to the ship, Miguel explains.

"The world is still searching for the 30 missing Hurley photographs."

"Who is Hurley?"

"The leader Shackelton's 1914 photographer on the attempt to reach the South Pole on the sailing ice-breaker Endurance."

"And,"

"When it was clear the pack ice had started to crush the ship, Hurley repeatedly dove into the sinking ship rescuing as many of his photo plates as he could. When the ship went under, 500 saved were piled up on the ice. When Shackleton organized the rescue plan, he and Hurley chose 150 of the best and smashed the rest so no one would be tempted to sneak more aboard the rescue boat they would need to drag across the ice by hand."

"So?"

"In the chaos of WWI, the Spanish flu, and the destroyed economies a century ago, only 120 images showed up after the rescue. No one knows where the 30 went – left on the Ice? Stolen in the celebrations of the rescue? Each year I dive in search of those which might have been left on the ice, and gradually, as pack ice will, shifted them into the Weddell Sea here..."

"Wow. I'm honored Miguel, to join your search."

With that we spend a grueling day, quick-dive light-searching for rectangular aberrations on the sea floor, shooting back up and running to the dry land to recover. On land, the legs especially for the first few minutes think they are extremely warm—the way the body heals itself with coursing blood flow after the minutes of those frigid water assaults—and the whole being has a racing sense of exhilaration, the adrenaline reaction. But it's no fun, for sure.

"Appreciate your pitching in," Don Miguel sends thanks my

way. "I see the Zodiac already coming for us."

"I'm so exhausted, I just want to bathe and go to sleep."

"Can't do. You need energy for our next two days' task. You did say you wanted to experience the authentic Antarctica, didn't you?"

So after dinner, I take the floor again on our Secrets game.

DAY TWO. Donna Story 1: I Am a Human Algorithm

When my school tested what career I should be good at, counselors discovered I had only one future-marketable skill— "Pattern Recognition." Short of turning into a machine, there was no known career at that time I could seek. I experimented privately and learned it is useful for survival. I can figure out how living things and institutions exhibit patterns that other people cannot see. I am able to communicate using patterns of my own to nudge events to protect and sometimes to even help me. No one knows how to imitate my algorithm. The End

"Madame Maccoy, that's not unbelievable nor even exaggerated. That's how things work."

"No it's not. People use violence or cowardice to change things, which doesn't disrupt the pattern. The pattern just wiggles a little, then reverts back to what I can try to change."

"Try again, please, Donna. It's elementary—we both know how to work it. Don't bore me."

DAY TWO. Donna Story 2: I Can Disappear Without Using Magic

As a toddler on the streets, dogs scared me. I hoped somebody—a magician—would make me invisible. It never happened. So I figured out my own magic tricks. If I was very still, and quiet, as if I were a tree, dogs would come to me and sniff and sometimes even pee. If I pretended I was invisible, they would get bored and go away. When years later I got my corporate job, I figured out ways to be so invisible that I would not be harmed. I was plain looking but neat, efficient, and unobtrusive. Other girls wore makeup and flirtatious clothes. Bosses' wives and lovers watched those rivals but never hounded me. This way I was able to advance, get more pay, and even accompany the bosses on business trips because I was invisible to those with power to stop me–jealous women who own their partners. The End

Don Miguel lets out such a laugh it would, as they say, wake the dead. "Why you manipulative scoundrel! I know there is something I like about you. Unfortunately, it's not the real you, I suspect. You confessed to be on a 2-week break, a devil-may-care explosion of fun and adventure."

"Not so fast, *Mister* de Casas. Who's to say if what I see before me is the real you? You pretty much did the same, saying Antarctica for 2 weeks was your chance to unwind. We're both performers."

He points to the *el acuerdo* bracelet on my wrist, leans toward me and kisses my forehead. "Now it's my turn to tell you two stories. You will choose the truth."

DAY TWO. Miguel Story 1: I Am a Human Internet.

As an adolescent, I found myself homeless in Buenos Aires. At first, I danced male-with-male Milongas for centavos, but as I grew older, I wanted to thank God for giving me life by doing what he rescued me to do. I grew so tall it was obvious a little Milonga street toy was not his intent. When I became a professional troupe dancer, the office would use me to carry private accountings to the silent owners. They liked that I never learned to write so the only way I could spill their secrets was to speak—and if necessary, I could always be shot before talking. Word spread how useful a messenger I could be.

"Oh my God, Miguel." I stop him with the "Too dangerous for me to know" signal, the snapped head and hand arc.

"Too late, Donna. I checked out where you learned the signal. We are tainted with the same profession."

I sigh and he continues.

As a popular performer who could be discreet while privately soothing any identity and mode of sex, and even throw in bestiality or whatever deviation was required, I was welcomed to cafes, *clubs, restaurants, networks, high-level meetings—overhearing information I could trade for $pesos, not centavos, and be trusted to do so safely for all. Eventually I had enough local backers to convert an abandoned mansion into my El Cuartel. Soon I gained international banking and government clients. On the Internet, you can FIND information with a search, but it cannot divulge secrets on its own. So I am a human internet. The End.*

"Granted, Don Miguel, this is interesting. But it is supposed to be short and not a confession, like you just gave. A game has rules. So please do better on your second story for **What is your special skill or talent?**"

DAY TWO. Miguel Story 2. Endurance.
Endurance changed my life. The End.

"Don Miguel, that's not one bit funny. We are only two days into the Secrets game."

"You will learn my Endurance story before we leave Antarctica."

"You are ruining the game."

"My not-so-invisible-partner, if I explain 'Endurance' now, I'll need to tell the secret of Mrs. Chippy. For that I'm not ready."

CHAPTER 14

DAY 3 SECRETS
Miguel Speaking

In the morning, I direct Donna what to bring today. "Of course you'll wear your red jacket and outer clothes and boots, but also roll your red dress—that thin knit fabric won't wrinkle this way —and throw it and your tango shoes into the bag with your crampons and pee jar."

"You're kidding."

"As I said, Donna. When I promise, you can count on me."

She watches as I put on my tuxedo under my outer wear and throw my patent slip-ons into my crampon and pee-jar bag.

After the Zodiac lands us on Lindblad Cove Beach, we crampon up and start our hike. She seems bewildered where we are hiking, so I prompt her. "What's your topic for tonight's Secrets game?"

"It's **When or how did you discover sex?**

"*Imirá vos*! Wow, Donna. You couldn't have dreamed up something more appropriate."

She blushes.

"I was invited a month ago to this party." I decide to tease her like when we first met. "Now we can party with the Adélies in style."

She knows by now not to believe everything I say when I try to cheer her and laughs, "Where's the real – as you say, the authentic Antarctica party?"

"Vernadsky Research Station."

"And,"

"After WWII, the Brits gave it away for a pound to Ukraine after having built it in the 1940s in case any Nazis decided to invade Antarctica. Now every year I report to Buenos Aires that all's well in Argentina's oversite of the station on our part of Antarctica. Meanwhile, each Friday the researchers there have information sharing with their government, after which they have a party where all are required to dress. We schedule my annual visit with their info-call which I join with them too. And of course, it's one helleva party after that yearly call."

"Wow. If true, it's really special I'll be with you tonight."

Hours later, we finally reach south on the "beak" and connect with their Zodiac to scoot us onto their island. Between the *laskavo prosymo, lyubyy Mihele, a khto tse?* (Welcome dear Miguel, and who is this?) *druh* (a friend) and *do horilky vvecheri p'yatnytsi!* (to Friday night vodka!), we make the government phone call, always a bit worrying because the limited war continues on their southeastern front since 2014. Except we tonight on the call pick up new more ominous now coded messages, things that can't be helped from here. The routine party is what's needed to feel their country, God willing, can avoid what is revealed.

Donna and I perform the Zotto I taught her. Between shots of *horilky* at the upstairs bar, built by the Brits like a real pub, everybody every which way *Milonga* cruising downstairs, Donna is seeing the most unusual station on Antarctica, yet crazily authentic of a slice of life down here. As with a *Milonga* hustle, everyone keeps going until the wee hours collapse them onto anything sleep-able.

"Quickly, Donna. Before we too collapse, let's go outside where it's private and do our Secrets game there."

DAY THREE. Donna Story 1: My First Grade Lover

When I was 6 years old, I went to school and fell in love with my new best girlfriend. Every recess we would sit outside together and hug and sometimes kiss. We didn't know we were doing something wrong. But Mother Superior saw us and brought us to her office. My friend said she didn't like me, that I forced her. So she went back to the classroom. I was whipped and all that year Sister Anesia would hit me with her ruler and make me sit in front of the class wearing a sign "Wicked Sinner." The nuns kept saying, we need to beat interest in girls out of you – do you hate girls now? The beatings didn't do it, but when my girlfriend stuck her tongue out at me, that's when I understood girls could be evil and I no longer wanted anything to do with them. The beatings didn't reform me, my chosen herself derailed my natural leaning. The End

"My poor Donna, I am so sorry to hear this."

"Don't jump to conclusions, remember this story might not even be true."

"There are bits about you that make me suspect it's true. You live amongst men and act as if women don't exist – if anything, you ignore – even scorn them —as incompetent boobs."

"Well stop suspecting what you don't know. If you want to hear about an incompetent boob, listen to my second story."

DAY THREE. Donna Story 2: A Baton and a Candle Stole My Virginity

My grandfather Maccoy rescued me from the druggies and took me to his ranch in Ireland to recover from the beatings the nuns rained on me. I begged him for a baton to twirl in the St Patrick's Day parade. I taught myself how to twirl and spin it, but when it came to passing it through my legs, I stumbled and fell onto it poking me in between. It hurt a lot but eventually I forgot about it. Meanwhile, because there was only an outhouse, I used to hold in my pee at night until morning. I found it gave me a delicious sensation that I'd enjoy until I had to quickly run to the privy. That early morning sensation got even better when I discovered I had a hole I could carefully insert the end of a candle into and move it in and out and around. At church I would silently thank Jesus and his father God for making human bodies so nice. When I returned to New York, I decided I was old enough to get rid of my virginity so I could thereafter see what sex was all about. A man who used to hang around agreed to help, but after a single insertion he was angry – what kind of fool do you think I am. You're not a virgin. I was dumbfounded. Today I realize the baton and a candle stole my virginity. The End

"More than likely, Donna, it was the candle. In traditional Japan, a man who purchased a child geisha's virginity, prepared her over many months by fingering and gradually stretching her opening with raw egg white coated fingers…"

"Well, you are still going to have to decide which is the true story. I'm ready to hear yours."

DAY THREE. Miguel Story 1: My Best 5 Years of Love

With the Pampas nuns, I didn't know love – each one was a bride of Jesus so they were overflowing with love for him, but none for me. When Padre Marcelo bought me, he became my guardian and surrounded me with his love. With him, we didn't have sex – he had vowed celibacy to become a Jesuit and I didn't need sex. I needed love. We would kiss and stroke our bodies and love. We never penetrated anywhere but marveled at the beauty of the male nude body. I lived and traveled with him on investigations the Provincial needed. As before, I remembered everything I read or was told, so I was a helpful assistant to Padre. There was no reason for me to learn to write – Padre wrote down the few things the Provincial needed to be told. England and Argentina, as you may know, have been fighting for centuries who has the valid claim to Antarctica, so we were sent to England to investigate the early explorers' archives. That is where I learned about Shackleton's Endurance and Mrs. Chippy. We Jesuits made enemies just by being in England, investigating. When I was 11, our bedroom was broken into when we were loving. The bobbies took pictures. I was returned to Buenos Aires and let loose on my own. The Padre was defrocked and caged in London gaol. That was the end of my best 5 years of love. The End

"I'm glad, Miguel, that you had some real love and affection before you were 11. I hope your son has a happier time now, than you did as a child."

"My son? Oh, that young man in Miami."

"Not your son?"

"My life partner, Luis-Alfonso. I try to give him a loving life."

DAY THREE. Miguel Story 2: I become Chippy

When I landed alone in Buenos Aires, I realized I'd need to invent myself – I didn't even have a name. I picked Chippy to start because that's what Padre used to call me when we were loving. I saw people dancing in the street and copied what they were doing. When I became good enough to be noticed, people wanted to dance with Chippy—mostly men, but some women too. I held my hand out for tips, and often my hand would take me to a room, a dark corner on the street, the back of a store where all sorts of sex brought me $pesos. Everyone knew Chippy was a good deal, discreet and amiable for anything. Because I much preferred love, I didn't mind doing sex for tips, big or small. That's how I discovered sex – a business proposition, nothing more, nothing less. And certainly nothing to give up loving for. The End

"Miguel, if you had no name, how did you come up with Miguel de Casas?"

"I needed a name I could aspire to when I stopped being Chippy. This is what I read: 'Saint Michael is an archangel, a spiritual warrior in the battle of good versus evil. He is considered a champion of justice, a healer of the sick, and the guardian of the Church. In art Saint Michael is depicted with a sword, a banner, or scales, and is often shown vanquishing Satan in the form of a dragon.' So I picked Miguel."

"Hey, you memorized that—you still don't know how to write?"

"Of course. That's what makes me valuable to those who need to move information—my messages are invisible."

And "de Casas"?

"When I purchased *El Cuartel*, I needed a legal name to be printed next to my X signature. I foolishly thought I should have many houses. Quickly I realized I could safely control and work out of only one house, but the deed was already official."

"Yes—I figured you had an assumed name. I even thought when I got home to check a secret list of elites who could be pinched for 'investments'..."

"As I said, Madame Maccoy, we're tainted by the same profession..."

CHAPTER 15

DAY 4 SECRETS
Donna Speaking

When I awaken, I realize that 24 hour sun is in the wrong place to be early morning. "Miguel. Wake up. We don't want to miss that Zodiac pickup, right?"

"Don't worry. They know about the annual party and will give us slack. They won't leave Antarctica without us."

"Is that what's next? Leaving Antarctica? I thought there was one more day."

"Both of us are right. There's one more day. Except technically, it won't be on Antarctica but in the South Shetland Islands." Miguel explains.

"Another one of those bait-and-switch ploys? Sheesh! This is ridiculous."

"But you aren't, Donna. You really do want to live in truth, even though you don't live truth, do you?"

I have to laugh, he's right. "Touché. The topic for tonight's stories is: **What is your life mission or goal?**"

After the weary 8-hour hike back to Lindblad Cove Beach, the Zodiac pickup and dinner, I once again start the game.

DAY FOUR. Donna Story 1: My goal is to see and learn everything.

Here on this planet, I presume I have only one chance to check it out. So, I want to learn from its earliest conception to its presence today. To see, experience, explore, not just things, but whatever species of life remain–I want to meet and if possible, love everything. The End.

"But Donna, you know that's impossible."

"Maybe, but who's to say I can't live forever? Meanwhile, I browse through writings through time. It lets me imagine all of this place..."

DAY FOUR. Donna Story 2: To find my phantom lover

When I was young and forbidden to love girls, I imagined what sort of man I could possibly be attracted to. It started slowly – I knew I preferred a skin less pinky-white than mine, eyes and hair should be deep brown, very tall and skinny like me...gradually as I added enjoyments to my own life, I added these to my phantom man – he should be a professional dancer, he should read and be curious, things like that. One day as I examine this man I imagine, I fall in love. Now I begin again to pleasure myself, not with any penetration, but rubbing my outer cluster of nerves. Every day I am happy and thrilling, imagining I am with my phantom love. I still miss the appeal of girls, but this phantom man I can sincerely love as well. I now know happiness I never thought I could find. Today I am still seeking this lover to be real, a living actual person to accept this yearning love. The End

"Donna, I don't know what to think—"

"Don't think. I found one love, my son Bruce's father, I thought was close enough but was killed in the 9/11 attack. I took that as a Black Swan message that I need to find someone **exactly** like my phantom lover for him not to be quickly destroyed. Sadly, Miguel, I never imagined him with a scar or a posse."

DAY FOUR. Miguel Story 1: To Use Information for Good.

Just as you, Donna, I seem to have a special skill—to whit, I can remember everything and recall at will. I profit. Business is business, so I don't feel it is wrong. But as I become more involved with other peoples and nations, I see despair. I begin to deposit information that can heal those who suffer. For example, when survivors from a tsunami need emergency aid, I message those with power and resources exactly who should organize the rescue for efficiency and lack of corruption; also, which indolent front man may take the credit for the humanitarian etc etc. I'm never a part of these missions, yet I can keep an eye on the front man and control him or her with a well-placed word everyone hears but does not remember where it came from. I keep up my performance of the gay man about town, always available for a good time and probably lacking the smarts to be threatening. This is how I keep myself and this goal safe. My mission is to secretly find and fix. The End.

"Interesting. My front man is always a top executive, boardroom level, and I'm brought along to keep him informed of what's really going on, as I pretend to be his not-too-bright Personal Assistant helper—we pretend ignorance of the language that I've been coached in, so we get to hear what they are really saying, thinking us trapped in business English. I'm present at all functions, official or not. But there's never an altruistic mission involved. Only business. No morals. Just money, unseen power."

DAY FOUR. Miguel Story 2: To Thwart our Species' cruelty—Mrs Chippy.
If you look at our history as an animal species, we have a strong urge to destroy each other. This has caused us to gather together into groups for safety and to make war. Many individuals have a natural urge to love and protect; others have a natural urge to devise and execute cruel punishments. When I read the Shackleton Diaries with Padre Marcelo, we learned that the ship's carpenter brought his beloved pet cat on board—all the Endurance crew loved that cat and played with it, and they jokingly renamed it "Mrs. Chippy" because she followed her owner wherever he went. Unfortunately, his owner was a mean uptight bastard, who loudly complained that many of the sailors were too friendly, that this was obscene, that it needed to be rooted out. When the ship was crushed by the Ice and sank, the carpenter staged a mutiny. After Shackleton put down the overthrow, he punished the carpenter by forcing him to shoot Mrs. Chippy because "the survivors need to save any remaining food rations for the humans." So although London heralded the explorers'

safe return, those explorers grieved for Mrs. Chippy, who through no fault of her own, was destroyed because she was an available tool for punishment. My goal is to prevent this kind of cruelty in war and power conflict. The End.

"You too, Miguel, were an accident, an available tool in the punishment his enemies rained down on your Padre."

"I don't do punishment." He turns his back and I watch him shudder, quake. Returning to me, he whispers "Remember?"

I can only look into his eyes, regretting my cruel accusation over the red dress....

"Donna, because we agreed that I would be leader on Day Five, I choose the topic — **What is our future?**"

CHAPTER 16

DAY 5 SECRETS
Miguel Speaking

Yes, the Swan Hellenic Vega leaves Lindblad Cove Beach early morning and heads north toward Argentina.

"Donna, climb up with me on the Swan's Nest observation post high—higher, I'll hold you on the edge of the prow — and you'll see something amazing."

"It looks like a giant brown upside-down bottlecap floating out there."

"Deception Iland, Donna. It's a live volcano, erupted blowing off part of a mountain 10,000 years ago. It's still active, erupted again in 1970, crushing all the buildings left by last century's whalers."

As the ship turns toward the brown cliffs, Donna calls "Oh my God, we're going to crash into it" jumps down and sits fetal position.

"Look, Donna, there's an entrance, albeit very narrow—Neptune's Bellows—that a really good captain navigates into the caldera lake. Swan Hellenic's, needless to say, are among the best. I've asked him to get us close to the black magma sand beach so the Zodiac can shuttle us there.

"What are those steamy things?"

"Fumaroles—vents in the surface of live volcanoes which spout. But here because the whole top collapsed into this undersea caldera, the fumaroles flood too and the water in them comes up to 70 degrees or more. So much nicer than when we were diving for Hurley's lost photo plates on the beak itself."

"You mean we're going to swim here? Should I wear my wet

suit under my outer clothes and boots? I didn't think to bring a swimming suit on this tour."

"Fumaroles are better *au naturel*. Remember when we were supposed to hold each other to keep from rolling off the floor-cushions when we took shifts sleeping in that Drake Passage storm. I can report, Donna, that when your sleeping mind was out in panic land, your body was alive and well and actively aroused my body holding yours."

After being dropped off at the magma beach, she notices the aberration of a shallow rough-dug indent partway into the water's edge. "What's that?"

"Check the internet. You'll find promotional images of giddy tour groups sitting in this water —swimsuits of course —like happy children at a beach about to build sandcastles. But they don't stay long – the caldera water is still cold, only the top handful of inches are warm and the deep is near freezing. It's really just another tourist photo-opt. Not the authentic life here."

"Which is,"

"The fumaroles. I know the good ones." I guide her to the sloping fumaroles field and pick out my favorite.

"Let me test it first." I strip and lower myself into the warm nearly 5-foot deep water-filled cylinder. I wave out my arms, inviting her to me...

She removes one thing after another, so different from her *gaucho* explosive stripping escapade. Now she slowly ballet walks nude and sits on the edge folding her knees so her legs are in the fumarole water too. I reach out and carry her light body into the water with me. I kiss the *acuerdo* bracelet she even sleeps with.

For a long time, we simply feel and relish each other in blissful *frottage*. Not with hands or fingers, but whole body, twisting and turning and body rubbing into each other, enjoying and heavily breathing in our delight.

"Miguel, it's a long story but a while ago I swore off full intimacy with anyone or anything. And I still won't allow it."

"Donna, I never wanted that kind of intimacy with you. Like with Marcelo, I don't need sex, I need your loving, the rapture."

Now we embrace. Chastely I suppose you'd call it, our bodies fitting together as best as our un-padded starvation-slim bones can manage.

"Miguel, you told me about your Mrs. Chippy. Would you like to hear about my cat Goldie?"

I don't answer. I'm ecstatic and don't care what she wants to tell me.

"Well, Miguel, when I swore off fully paired intimacy, I used a vibrator to pleasure myself with my cluster of nerves down there. It takes practice, and imagining my phantom lover, to tip into climax. My pet cat Goldie would come near to watch and one day when I was getting close, she lept onto my chest and dug her claws into my collarbone. That threw me right then into ecstasy."

I'm still beyond speaking.

"Miguel, if you would be my Chippy, I'll be your Goldie."

I turn her around and press my body into her back, taking the heel of my palm around her and work it into her lower nerve center there. She spins around my demanding palm heel, moaning right and left, up and down until she shudders and stiffens, sighing my name Miguel. Now she whips around and captures my back with her body, doing the *Zotto Milonga* kick I taught her, but not gently through splayed legs from the front, but strongly from the back, lifting her left leg until she hits my lower pelvic bone shifting my parts higher yet. Then she wraps her arm around to my front, and with the heel of her palm, traces a deep winding path along my scar, collarbone to belly. My erection explodes feeding the warm water and I hear "It's Marcelo. We both love you."

We slowly recover and realize we have at last reached the *el acuerdo*, The Understanding.

Still soaking in the warm fumarole, I descend to earth and whisper, "Since this is my leader day, Donna, we should finish our Secrets game before the Zodiac comes to pick us up. You always go first . **What is our future?**"

DAY FIVE. Donna Story 1: I'm a Reluctant Spy and Have an Assignment After the Tour.

When I was forced to be available for assignments to replace my husband's failure to protect, I thought the Cold War being over, I'd never actually be called for duty. Not true. The captain told me at breakfast this morning there's a detained American journalist in an exchange agreement for one of theirs, a mathematician they need back. Trouble is, the mathematician and his wife slipped into New York City five years ago and disappeared. That was the whole message, so sadly, I'm being tapped for duty, Don Miguel. I can't play anymore. I need to go back and find this mathematician. The End.

"Donna, there was never any expectation of us playing together in the future—we were upfront that we were each on a 2-week let-loose play break."

"As you say."

"Normally I would offer to help you find who you will be looking for, but it seems you have been purposely put in ridiculous danger. The captain would have gained the information and been instructed to deliver it to you, through ship electronics–so now your name and assignment are spreading throughout the dark world."

"Seriously?"

"Donna, YOU need help. But we need to talk cleverly – away from electronics, gossipy people—here on Deception is the ideal spot. First, who knew you were on your way to Antarctica?"

"Just my husband, but I gave him no details, only that I was on my way to Antarctica."

"That was enough – if someone astute calls your home asking for you, just the word *Antarctica* is enough to figure out which tour."

"My husband was never astute enough…"

"Neither were you, Donna. You should have told him you were on your way to Zambia–or the moon, as a smartass dead-end answer, especially if you know your husband is too oblivious to protect you."

"That's why I had to get involved to prevent another assassination of his refugee friends—but that's another story and I guess I'm learning the hard way, self-taught by doing and messing it up."

"OK, here's some training from another self-taught, but I've lived probably 20-odd years more than you, so here's Lesson 1. Always, even before danger arises, **devise a plan A and a plan B, if A quickly fails.** For you now, A: When you get home, play dumb —make up anything—that you never made it to the tour, missed your flight, whatever. But if you detect you are being hunted, then do B —hide out for a while—can you?"

"Yes, there are some under-the-radar private retreats in New Jersey my husband used to frequent when he did his erotic paintings. They're camouflaged as boring private health clubs. The less easy part of hiding is making an airtight excuse why I'm not at my desk but I'll make it work. Somehow."

"Good girl. Let's get on with our Secrets game before the Zodiac comes to pick us up."

DAY FIVE. Donna Story 2: I grieve for Milonga
I already grieve for no longer sharing a Milonga life with you. The End.

"Donna, I feel sorry too, especially since you feel I missed the boat because the lover you imagined didn't have a scar and a posse living in his barracks, but your thrilling and my thrilling, even though neither of us wants fully intimate sex together, cannot be dismissed. Different from what I feel for the males I'm naturally attracted to, yet it's still real. We cannot ignore it—or each other. In some way and some place, we will be together. Don't grieve. When you miss happiness, dance the *Zotto* I taught you, hear the music in your head and let your body feel me partnering..."

"And your stories for our future?"

DAY FIVE. Miguel Story 1: I Am Married and Must Repair My

Partnership.

When I reached age 55, I convinced myself I was ready for a love partner, like Padre and I had been. I found a compatible young man Luis-Alfonso and we married. But this marriage does not have the magic that I had with Marcelo. Two days before the tour that we routinely take each year, as I climaxed, I unexpectedly – to me as well as him—called out "Marcelo". As you can imagine, that caused such an angry rift that he refused to accompany me to Antarctica. That's how, first on the waiting list, you became my replacement cabinmate. Now I must repair my marriage, help it become a more true partnership. The End.

"So you too are in a May-December marriage—they don't seem to work out so well," she sighs.

"That's the *non-sequitur* of the ages, Donna.

"Miguel, I've been honest and open with you. For all those years since Marcelo, did you imagine who you could love?"

"Of course. A man, but not so much a man as a man-child. Sort of like you are years-wise clearly an adult woman, but you still think and act and react like the child you once were."

"No, Miguel, I rescued the forgotten child in me when I realized I had rescued everybody else and could now stop being so in-charge. But don't you see? My phantom lover was nearly like you, but not close enough. And I am nearly like what you can love, but I'm not a man. We both came close but still missed the boat."

"Donna, perhaps God created this place where nothing can be perfect and he challenges us, also his creations, to figure out how to make it work."

DAY FIVE. Miguel Story 2: I Will Find and Always Love You.

We must both go back to our established lives, Donna, but sometime, somewhere, some place I will find and love you always. The End.

"Don Miguel, all my stories were true."

"As mine." I touch her lips.

The pickup Zodiac beaches on Deception.

"Quickly Donna, before we board. At Vernadsky, I learned of a sad development in their nation— the country will be invaded, attacked before July 1. The squad will meet me in Ushuaia and we will all travel together to Miami but will no longer talk because ears are everywhere now."

The Zodiac reaches the ship ladder, and we climb back to our imperfect lives.

CHAPTER 17

FOUND
Donna Speaking

Back on board the Swan Hellenic Vega, I am thankful for Drake Lake calm seas as we return to Ushuaia. We spend our last time together in our little basement room, longing, loving. Feeling our bodies together, all. We turn up twice for dinner, and choose the most secluded table to be alone even to dine.

After the last dinner, Miguel motions me out onto the Swan's Nest observation post and whispers, "I haven't engraved your son's money clip gift, and won't – here, Donna, toss it into the sea. Understand you are now a pariah for him. Separate yourself from Bruce and his Air Force career."

I catch my breath, not sure I hear him right.

"Reconnect after he retires."

I stare at him, trying not to believe, but I know he's right. "I am grateful for this Lesson 2."

As we exit the ship at Port Ushuaia, Miguel again whispers "I will be near you, my soul will find yours no matter where each one of us will be. Look for me in your quiet moments and your dreams..."

After the 4-hour jaunt to Buenos Aires, and the 8-hour flight to Miami, he whispers he has upgraded my ticket to New York, and to collect it at the check-in kiosk. We separate.

I see over by the VIP Lounge, Miguel is joined by his Luis-Alfonso, and along with the bodyguards, the group disappears inside.

Now that we are apart, I am alone. Lost. On the plane back

to JFK, I am stoic in the 3-hour flight home. I prepare for the challenges ahead.

But when I open the window shutter and see off in the distance, the silhouette of the city's skyscraper lights cutting through the black midnight sky, I can't be stoic anymore. I quietly sob, wiping away the tears with my fingers. I taste their saltiness and find no comfort.

The plane lands and I re-enter life as it is.

After the late-night cab ride, I open the apartment door.

As always, David has all the lights turned on.

Goldie, my cat, comes to greet me as she always does when I come home from work.

I wait for Tanya, who effectively is a part-time care-giver of my 80-odd year-old husband David. When she comes, I shush her. "Just stay with him. I'll take the daybed..." Caregiver or not, Tanya has always been the love of his life and I know fear of the dark is not his only injury.

I revive my daily routines. As I do at home, instead of a sleeping pill, I relax before going to bed with a glass of Cabernet Sauvignon. I tease myself with the thought, Donna, should you switch now to Argentine Malbec? No, it was a fun time, but that exciting life was never mine, just a two-week gift from Don Miguel. I sip the deep red potion and realize that I'll probably never wear that red dress again. As I put the half-drunk glass in the refrigerator—I really must go to sleep now —I muse how ironic it is that I just returned from Antarctica with 24-hour daylight, when here at home, that's how we always live.

Dozing off, I feel something soft rub my bare ankle. A slender black cat has appeared on the daybed – I tell it, "I don't know where you came from, but you can have a home here too. I'll call you "Found."

Unexpectedly flooding my soul, the Gaelic Sound of Silence tune *Fonn Na Saoirse* my Grandfather Maccoy used to sing, fills me with yearning.

Then I know. This isn't "Found"—its name is *Fonn–Desire*.

I touch the *el acuerdo* bracelet. Miguel has kept his promise; his soul has found mine. Yes, we are together. I smile.

Suddenly I'm startled by a gentle shaking of my shoulder. It's Tanya, leaving. "I'm sorry to wake you, but before I go, a man came yesterday looking for you. Asked if you know a mathematician to tutor someone. When I told him you weren't here, he said to tell you he'll be back."

Oh my God, I'm already being hunted in my dark world assignment. I remember so well Miguel's plan B for me. Shocked to be hunted so soon, I know I can't delay finding the object of this search, to be done with it and never be hunted again…

I gather my resolve to brave the quest and pray for guidance and strength . My soul reaches out to his soul, to Don Miguel.

Now the search ahead will turn out to be another adventure, of that I am sure. I smile.

◆ ◆ ◆

https://www.annalonzobooks.com
ann@annalonzobooks.com
annalonzobooks@gmail.com

ACKNOWLEDGEMENT

I wish to acknowledge and thank collaborator and co-writer **Merlin Edward Angel**, designer extraordinaire and infinitely knowledgeable, who not only designs visual creations and arrangements perfectly spot-on in real time, but also shares his parallel gift of words to create compelling yet still romantic challenges for the characters in these bi romances. With all his visual gifts, Edward is also the consummate story editor as well as text and word editor. The novella would not have happened were it not for this "Angel" willing to share his skills and sophistication in the creation of these projects.

And thank you **Andrew Martinez**, founder of **Powerful Digital Solutions**, (*powerfuldigitalsolutions.com*), who so adroitly handles my web site and more, sharing his massive command of digital world tech processes along with his personal experience as author of his own books. How wonderful I met you through the zoom topic "Essential Graphic Design Skills for Authors in the Digital Age" you gave in May 2024 to **Romance Writers of America's LERA** chapter.

I am grateful to mathematician/political theorist **Nassim Nicolas Taleb** (*https://fooledbyrandomness.com/*) whose recognition and comprehensive development of his Black Swan effect, triggered particularly by the 9/11 attack on New York City, set the stage for the Black Swan symbol I've used in this novella and the others in this series.

And without **Swan Hellenic Expedition Ships'** (*https://www.swanhellenic.com/ship/vega-2*) newly designed luxury cruise fleet with their unique "Swan's Nest Observation" prow deck on **SH Vega**, we could not experience the rapture of the "Black Swan" reaching into the Drake storm's windswept maelstrom. As Taleb has posited, "Remember that you are a Black Swan."

Professionally, I acknowledge the writer critique groups who have given generous and helpful feedback on drafts. In that sense, **The Floridita Queer Writers Club**, Fort Lauderdale, Fl, founded by **Neil M. Frau-Cortes (*www.neilfrau.com*)**, script writer/series designer **Douglas Haines (*rdouglashaines@gmail.com*)** and others, has been of invaluable support.

Read! Write! Critique! zoom group, hosted by the Palm Beach County Public Library System, group managed by writer **Karen M. Crisco,** and those others in this critique group including author **Jeffrey Hammerhead Philips (*jeffreyphilips.com*)**, with published mystery novels of sea diving and Cherokee lore, who has generously served as my astute creative writing mentor, helping me graduate out of those horrible "first tries" at fiction. **Lori Flynn (*loriflynn.net*) (*lorfly@gmail.com*)**, published romance suspense author, who encouraged me always, especially saying "Don't worry, you'll rewrite that first chapter a thousand times as you develop your story."

My first writer meetup group, **The Bards.** Members have since dispersed to become a zoom workshop under the thoughtful tutelage of **Carol K Howell**, award-winning short-story writer with published books Traffik Games, The Happy Sappersteins and, shortly, Gittel's Golem and Other Stories of Magical Realism. **Mary Ann Lonze**, now working on her second in "The Complex" sci-fi series, who charmed me with her memoir of a gay ESL Japan gardener she'd met and grew to understand. **Judith Blotnick**, a fellow New York writer, who pushed me to write my own memoirs, to figure out some way to avoid naming names and ending up in jail. Thank you, Judy, I needed your push and innate courage to get me going. **Mary King (*maryannaking.com*)** whose memoir "Bastards" gave me courage to face dysfunctional childhood and decide to grow from it, because of it. **Dr Meg Newman**, whose memoir-in-progress, shows that indeed one could fight back discrimination and follow the life nature intended, rather than hide and allow others to shape life according to mores that thwarted your genes and nature itself. And finally, please find the time to write again, **Monique Evans**. Who can ever forget your masterpiece short story "A Dog Called Perry" choosing life in poor Jamaica; your metaphor of survival at all costs encouraged me to keep writing.

I especially treasure the elegant gold and diamond delicate swan brooch my local Palm Beach supporters presented to me as a pre-launch visible signature to wear at events, readings, out and about, and whenever I share this novella with others. Look for it in my web site's welcome videos. It touches my soul, dear **Edward, Andy, Terry, Alex Z and Mario**.

Finally, I acknowledge this tribute to my longtime friend **Andy Casas**, who inspired me to create the generous go-getter "Don Miguel de Casas". Andy, it's a pleasure and an honor to work with you!

To all who contributed so much to this project, *Gracias*!

With love and gratefulness, Ann Alonzo

BI WANDERLUST ROMANCES BY ANN ALONZO

This series, currently planned for 5 volumes, features LGBTQ bi romances set in exotic, polar, and major cities locations with intriguing and provocative events and characters creating exciting stories. The series is made of short novellas, perfect for a pleasant read when you have a few hours to sit back and enjoy the adventures - and yes, the romance!

His Secret Academy

Set in New York City and art enclaves in the USA, with short missions in Canada and elsewhere. Lives upended by the attacks on the towers in 9/11, Donna Maccoy with David Knight, a Romanian spy on the run, make a marriage of convenience to rescue each other and promise the pact is forever. In the crazed ups and downs of New York City in the next decades, they try to make their facade hetero marriage work by any means available. Finally they come to a new understanding which enables Donna to win a ticket on a 5-star Antarctica tour leaving in 24 hours.

Their Tango And Antarctica Secrets

Set in Argentina, the stormy Drake passage between the continents, and Argentina's claimed right and control of their section of Antarctica. Donna Macoy is unexpectedly paired with mysterious man-about-town Buenos Aires "Porteño" Don Miguel de Casas who has been stood up by his partner Luis-Alfonso, leaving the fortunate Donna as first on the wait list to be awarded that place in the tour. Thrown together, they grapple with undeniable attraction to each other, the memories of childhood feelings, and how can they go forward together while returning to their own imperfect lives. Donna is tapped to find a foreign spy through her marriage agreement, leading to the next adventure volume.

Naturally The Spy

Set in the naturist community in the East coast, USA, nude health and social clubs and their somewhat under-the-radar subculture. There's a detained American journalist in an exchange agreement for one of theirs, a mathematician they need back. Trouble is, the mathematician and his wife slipped into New York City five years ago and disappeared. Donna encounters various gender partners. Among these is an unknown French-Canadian physician who is in transformation, Don Miguel de Casas, Donna's Antarctica tour cabinmate. What more surprises await this spy hunt – is the tracked spy actually here?

The Mao Of Chinese Treasure

Set in the existing hoards of Chinese treasure – Manhattan, Washington DC, London, Berlin, Taipei, Beijing, Xi'an and the Yellow River, Donna and Miguel, no longer in disguise, team up to hunt for the missing Neanderthal pot dating from 20,000 years ago found in the Xianrendong Cave Jiangxi province. A shy male protector of the pot surfaces, and great conflict with unsought love occurs within the little search-and-find party...leading to an ending that propels readers to the 5th novella of the series.

The Bracelet Of Life Or Death

Set in Ecuador and the Galapagos Islands with Donna and especially Miguel dealing with political threats and retribution, Miguel introduces Donna to her long-lost love, the woman she fell in love with and was thwarted from loving when they were both schoolgirls – he searched the world for her and found her here pining also for her first love, girlfriend Donna. She is Miguel's gift to Donna after all they have been through together. He asks for the "el acuerdo" The Understanding, bracelet he gave her and that she never removes. In his embrace, together with her on a small dinghy, amongst the swimming seals and gregarious penguins, he breaks open the Bracelet of Life or Death and—

ARGENTINE SLANG AND A FEW WORDS TO KNOW

SHUSHING: Contrary to the rest of the Spanish speaking world, Argentinians, especially in the capital and leading cultural city Buenos Aires, speak what they call "shushing" where a Y before a vowel is pronounced "sh" like Yo is Sho. This goes for double L like street Calle is pronounced Cashe. Further, the single for "you" Tu is replaced with "Vos". And there are other sound permutations and complex grammar rules – but basically you should hear a lot of "Shushing". In fact, it was one way native Argentinians could tell who was a tourist or recent immigrant who hadn't yet picked up the local lingo.

PAYING IN ARGENTINA: Paying in American dollars was much preferred. Centavos during Argentina's galloping inflations were nearly worthless, but $pesos were valuable because they could be exchanged at a bank for American dollars, so largely stable and not as devalued by Argentina's inflation.

Porteño – People from Buenos Aires call themselves *Porteños* which means people of the major shipping port of the *Río de la Plata* river meeting the Atlantic Ocean in Buenos Aires.

Slang: *Mirá vos*!—I translated it as WOW. It literally means "You look" but as one slang sleuth said, you could spend all day listing how and when Argentinians say it…. In general, Argentine slang is blunt and earthy – in translation not polite at all, but the literal meanings have often been reversed into "we're friends so we can raz each other for fun and to show how close we are" – another way of building community...

Below are a few important words as you read. When necessary to understanding of less repeated words, I put the English word directly after the Spanish italics, but the following are important enough that if you forgot what they mean, here's a quick way to look them up alphabetically:

Agentinidad—what it means to be an Argentine, the national character and characteristics

el Acuerdo—understanding, a deeply personal meaning to understanding

Black Swan—an unexpected unpredictable high impact event or person that changes everything

el Cuartel—barracks

Facónes—large deadly knives used by gauchos in knife fights and protection, since they couldn't carry guns nor afford supplies of bullets sold only in towns where they could be captured.

Fonn (Irish Gaelic) - "Desire". Used in the Gaelic words of the Sound of Silence tune, *Fonn na Saoirse* as per TG Lurgan. In the Munster accent, it sounds like Frown or Down.

Gaucho—the Argentine cowboy on the Pampas plains, often renegade outlaws.

Maté—traditional herb drink in a personal small gourd shared with a single straw to create community. It is pronounced MAH-tay accent on 1st syllable

Milonga— the original African dance that evolved into the Tango-like dance today. *Porteños* continue to dance socially the complex machismo *Milonga* rather than the "watered down" Tango suitable for polite tourists.

LINKS IF YOU WANT TO GO THERE TOO

Chapter 1

Hotel Palacio, Buenos Aires *https://www.hyatt.com/en-US/hotel/ argentina/palacio-duhau-park-hyatt-buenos-aires*

Chapter 3

Plaza de Mayo in front of Presidential Palace *https:// turismo.buenosaires.gob.ar/en/otros-establecimientos/plaza- de-mayo* (also in Spanish)

La Recoleta Cemetery *https://turismo.buenosaires.gob.ar/es/ otros-establecimientos/cementerio-de-la-recoleta* (also in English)

Duarte Family Tomb containing Eva Perón *https:// www.buenosairesfreewalks.com/what-to-do/grave-of-evita- peron/*

Chapter 4

Raoul Wallenburg Memorial "Hero Without a Grave 1912 —", bronze by Beñat Iglesias Lopez, second floor Terminal A, Ezeiza airport. *https://www.raoulwallenberg.net/wallenberg/hero-without-grave/*

Chapter 5

Fogón Restaurant Gaucho Asada Style Buenos Aires – YUM! *https://fogonasado.com/*

Chapter 6

San Antonio de Areco Village https://areecotradicion.com/ en/ *https://arecotradicion.com/en* and *info_areco/the-town-and-*

its-history/

San Antonia de Areco Estancias *https://www.sanantoniodeareco.com/donde-dormir/estancias* (also in English)

Chapters 7 and 8

Milonga Tango – national pastime, here's a good intro but there are planty of web sites, blogs, magazines, books, teachers, events – ENJOY! *https://vamospanish.com/discover/tango-in- buenos-aires/*

Port Ushuaia radial prison from 1902 *https://www.wmf.org/project/ushuaia-prison* and *https://museomaritimo.com/en/museum-of-the-prison-of-ushuaia*

Beginning with Chapter 9-16

Swan Hellenic Expedition Ships' newly designed luxury cruise fleet with their unique "Swan's Nest Observation" prow deck with 360 degree view. The **Vega** is the ship used by this posh Antarctica Tour *https://www.swanhellenic.com/ship/vega-2*

Chapter 14

Vernadsky Research Station. Yes you can visit it - Today, the scientists conducting research open their doors so that travelers can understand what it is they do, and appreciate what a working scientific Antarctic base is like. The base is also home to the **southernmost bar in the world, the Faraday bar**, and **a post office** so that you can send a postcard memento to all your loved ones from Antarctica! There are lots of web sites mentioning this base, but scroll down on this one from the Explorers' Club for a good intro: *https://www.secretatlas.com/ explorers-club/travel-tips/antarctica-travel-guide/*

Wishing you a great trip!

Your friend as always, Ann Alonzo

SOURCES

KEY SOURCES- In addition to my memories and diaries, and many other research books and web sites, these are some of the key sources I checked to make sure my memories were accurate as Ann Alonzo:

The new **Swan Hellenic Vega "Discovery" Cruise Ship** Donna and Miguel sail to Antarctica. Includes the Swan's Nest 360-degree Observation Platform with soaring black arch on the extreme prow of the ship, a unique feature only of the Swan Hellenic fleet. This 5-star luxury expedition ship incorporates elegant Scandi-design with the latest in cruising technology, and has a PC5 ice-strengthened hull, and extra-large stabilizers, to make the journey safe and as smooth as possible in the Drake Passage. *https://www.swanhellenic.com/*

MUSIC VIDEOS

Fonn Na Saoirse, Gaelic words of the Sound of Silence tune, *Fonn na Saoirse* as per TG Lurgan. *https://www.youtube.com/watch?v=6ZAGer1c-fI&list=RD6ZAGer1c-fI&start_radio=1*

Madonna Vogue, the official 1990 voguing video directed by David Fincher *https://www.youtube.com/watch?v=GuJQSAiODqI*

Zotto Milonga, Zotto dancing milonga at tango magia 15 *https://music.youtube.com/watch?v=_4GO3HpzArc*

BOOKS (BLACK SWAN)

Taleb, Nassim Nicholas. **INCERTO 5** Volume philosophical and practical essay on uncertainty (**Skin In the Game** 2018, **Antifragile** 2014 ,**The Black Swan** 2007, **Fooled by Randomness** 2005, and **The Bed of Procrustes** 2010), **Statistical Consequences of Fat Tails: Real World Preasymptotics, Epistemology, and Applications** (2023 Revised Edition) (Technical Incerto, STEM Academic Press) a (so far) 6-volume "investigation of opacity, luck, uncertainty, probability, human error, risk,and decision making when we don't understand the world, expressed in the form of a personal essay with autobiographical sections, stories, parables, and philosophical, historical, and scientific discussions in nonoverlapping volumes that can be accessed in any order." Random House, 1745 Broadway, New York NY 10019. USA

BOOKS (GENERAL):

Aymar, Brandt. **The Young Male Figure, In Paintings, Sculptures, and Drawings from Ancient Egypt to the Present.** 275 illustrations. 1970. Crown Publishers, Inc. 419 Park Avenue South, New York, NY. 10016. Currently out-of-print.

Burleson, William E. **Bi America: Myths, Truths, and Struggles of an Invisible Community.** 2005, 2014. Routledge, 711 Third Avenue, New York, NY 10017, USA. Isbn 978-1-560 23479-1

Ochs, Robyn & Rowley, Sarah E. **Getting Bi, Voices of Bisexuals Around the World.** Second Edition.2009. Bisexual Resource Center, PO Box 1026, Boston, Ma, USA 02117-1026, isbn 978-0-9653881-5-3

BOOKS (ARGENTINA):

Benson, Andrew & O'Brien, Rosalba. **The Rough Guide to Buenos Aires.** Second Edition. 2011. www.roughguides.com isbn 978-1-84836-891-0

Borges, Jorge Luis. **On Argentina.** 2010. Penguin Group USA. 375 Hudson Street, New York, NY 10014 USA. Isbn 978-0-14-310573-2

Elliott, David. **Argentina 1920-1994 Art from Argentina.** The Museum of Modern Art Oxford. 1994. Museum of Modern Art, Oxford. 30. Pembroke Street, Oxford, OX1 1BP. Isbn 0 905 836 87 1

Martínez, Tomás Eloy. **The Tango Singer.** 2004-2006. Bloomsbury Publishing Plc, 36 Soho Square, London W1D 3QY. Isbn 978-0-7475 8578 7

Vilaplana, Cynthia. **Argentine Spanish, A Guide to Speaking Like an Argentine, The Complete Lessons.** 2017. speakspanish@gmail.com isbn 978-1549941-412

BOOKS (ANTARCTICA): There are numbers of excellent books published recently, well worth reading. These are three of the most pertinent to this story.

Bound, Mensun. **The Ship Beneath the Ice, The Discovery of Shackleton's Endurance.** 2022. HarperCollins Publishers, 195 Broadway, New York, NY 10007. In the course of the story of the hunt for the ship sunk in the ice, he describes sea and wind conditions as they affect the discovery hunt.

Shackleton, Sir Ernest. **SOUTH, The Story of Shackleton's Last Expedition, 1914-17.** First published 1919 in Great Britain. 1991 edition edited by Peter King. Century Ltd., 20 Vauxhall Bridge Road, London SWIV 2SA. Shackleton's own account of the expedition; includes original photos; also an introduction on Shackleton's life and personality.

Young, Karen Romano. **Antarctica, the Melting Continent.** 2022. What On Earth Publishing, Allington Castle, Maidstone, Kent ME16 ONB, UK and 30 Ridge Road, Unit B, Greenbelt, Maryland, 20770, USA. Isbn 978-1-913750-53-4 Note- this is a slim book meant for middle school age readers, but loaded with the most current climate details as studied on site by this British researcher. Highly recommended. Ann Alonzo.

ANTARCTICA, DRAKE STORM VIDEOS

https://www.youtube.com/watch?v=kQFC6yhLvBA

https://www.youtube.com/watch?v=-xR5Ov6Sd4E

https://www.youtube.com/watch?v=iuMKDbtjFyQ&t=55s

BOOKS (INSIGHTS ON THE BRAIN CAPABILITIES OF DONNA & MIGUEL)

Baron-Cohen, Simon. **The Pattern Seekers, How Autism Drives Human Invention, a 70,000-year History.** 2020. Basic Books, Hachette Book Group. 1290 Avenue of the Americas. New York, NY 10104. USA. Isbn 978-1-5416-4714-5. Both Donna and Miguel employ pattern recognition.

Foer, Joshua. **Moonwalking with Einstein, The Art and Science of Remembering Everything.** 2011-2012. Penguin Group USA. 375 Hudson Street, New York, NY 10014 USA. isbn 978-0-14-312053-7. Describes the feats of memory recall possible in the human brain, using techniques used in the educated world before the invention of book printing. Miguel's ability to remember is real, not a "fairy-tale."

Grandin, Temple. **Visual Thinking, The Hidden Gifts of People Who Think in Pictures, Patterns, and Abstractions.** 2022. Riverhead Books. Penguin Random House LLC, penguinrandomhouse.com. isbn 978-0-593-41836-9.

WHY BI ROMANCES

Sound familiar...bi romances? I'd love to read them but they aren't so easy to find.

Why is that? Are we an untapped market because many of us aren't comfortably bi yet? Or is it because we're not too clear on what being bi is?

Sure, I can give you this pedantic word salad: *Being bi is the attraction or active relationship of one gender with pairs or groups of other genders, not limited to Male or Female, but can include any permutation out there. Sometimes even fluid combinations over time or place.*

But it's more intriguing to learn what bi can be through stories. There are so many ways in real life to follow each sensual turn or possibility to discover happiness.

I want to help launch a breakthrough genre with my bi romances, short novellas with each unique bi initiative being provocative— and yes, romantic.

I'm beginning with the memoir I've been asked to write but have always refused, reluctant to reveal my own escapades. Yet there's a way...I can rename to fictionalize the main characters and let the stories themselves unfold the action in each tempestuous and romantic bi episode. And with my Wanderlust descriptions and links in the back of this book to the actual places and luxury ship fleet, you too can explore these same exotic locations.

I invite you to join me here as I write about my heroine Donna's adventures with men, women and other genders she encounters in her exciting life.

Check my web site **https://annalonzobooks.com** often, join my email list **ann@annalonzobooks.com**, sit back and enjoy the adventures!

Your friend as always, Ann Alonzo

◆ ◆ ◆

https://www.annalonzobooks.com
ann@annalonzobooks.com
annalonzobooks@gmail.com

Made in the USA
Middletown, DE
08 September 2024

60278433R00064